"*The Job Loss Recovery Guide* is a practical guide for using the power of imagery to recover from the trauma of job loss by making new body-mind-spirit connections. Dr. Lynn Joseph's step-by-step strategies are easy to follow and will help you move quickly toward success and healing."

—Barbara M. Dossey, Ph.D., RN, Director, Holistic Nursing Consultants, Santa Fe, New Mexico, and author of *Rituals of Healing*

"A powerful program! Quickly take control of your future with this step-by-step job loss recovery program."

—Mikela and Philip Tarlow, authors of *Digital Aboriginal: The Direction of Business*

"People who have lost their jobs can feel profound fear and trepidation. Lynn Joseph's work is a true gift to them."

—Marianne Williamson, author of the New York Times bestseller *A Return to Love*

The
JOB-LOSS
RECOVERY
Guide

A PROVEN PROGRAM
FOR GETTING
BACK TO WORK—FAST!

LYNN JOSEPH, PH.D.

New Harbinger Publications, Inc.

Publisher's Note

This publication is designed to provide accurate and authoritative information in regard to the subject matter covered. It is sold with the understanding that the publisher is not engaged in rendering psychological, financial, legal, or other professional services. If expert assistance or counseling is needed, the services of a competent professional should be sought.

Distributed in the U.S.A. by Publishers Group West; in Canada by Raincoast Books; in Great Britain by Hi Marketing, Ltd.; in South Africa by Real Books, Ltd.; in Australia by Boobook; and in New Zealand by Tandem Press.

Copyright © 2003 by Lynn Joseph

New Harbinger Publications, Inc.
5674 Shattuck Avenue
Oakland, CA 94609

Cover design by Lightbourne Images
Edited by Carole Honeychurch
Text design by Michele Waters

ISBN 1-57224-353-8 Paperback

New Harbinger Publications' Web site address: www.newharbinger.com

05   04   03

10   9   8   7   6   5   4   3   2   1

First printing

Contents

Acknowledgements

This book materialized from my deep desire to share the tested and proven Job-Loss Recovery Program with exiting or displaced employees everywhere.

It would not have been possible to write it without the unwavering love and support of my husband, Neil. His belief in me is a continual motivation, and for that I am grateful.

I would like to thank Editor-in-Chief Matthew McKay, Ph.D., who believed in this book from the start. Thanks are also due to Senior Acquisitions Editor Tesilya Hanauer and Editor Carole Honeychurch at New Harbinger Publications. I could not have asked for more supportive professionals with whom to work.

Special thanks to my "book doctor" and friend, Shirl Thomas. Her skills and untiring standard of excellence are evident throughout this book.

I am also grateful for the comments and suggestions of my friend and colleague, Dorothea Hover-Kramer, Ph.D.

Finally, I gratefully acknowledge Melanie E. Greenberg, Ph.D., who, as my Dissertation Chair, expertly guided me through my doctoral research. Without her willingness to support my investigation of mental image technology, this book could not have come about.

Introduction

At age fifty-one, Rick was abruptly laid off from his job of three years as a manager in Systems and Technology. He entered my job-loss study after two months of unsuccessfully seeking reemployment. Immediately following the study, Rick wrote, "I was very fortunate to be a member of your study group . . . and I will always appreciate it. Your program addressed inner control and understanding, while allowing me to move past the emotional side of being laid off."

Less than two months later, Rick accepted a new position as a senior project manager; however, he e-mailed me eight months into his new job to say, "The company I went to work for has started major downsizing. My project and my entire department are being outsourced to India. This is business, and change is part of the game. Rest assured your program will help me address the challenge ahead."

Then it hit me. Downsizing wasn't just a temporary phenomenon. Corporate downsizing and restructuring had become common strategies designed to reduce expenses and increase profits and had resulted in significant employee displacement and transition. Exiting (displaced or laid-off) employees everywhere would need new tools to quickly take control of their careers. I was convinced I could provide those tools.

Where I'm Coming From

Let me back up a bit. When, in the third year of my doctoral studies, it became necessary to select a research topic for my dissertation, I gravitated toward a subject that had held my interest for many years: mental image technology. Mental imagery—you may also know it as creative visualization or guided imagery—is a thought process that consciously directs and focuses the imagination to create an internal experience. It includes the use of all five senses for maximum effectiveness: sight, sound, touch, taste, and smell.

Change, healing, and goal achievement can all happen quickly with the use of mental image technology, or MIT, as I call it. I knew this to be true from the research I'd done on the technique, and from having experienced its seeming magic in my own life.

Once I selected my doctoral research topic, I needed an application on which to test it. I ultimately chose reemployment for three reasons.

- If MIT were found effective in decreasing landing time after job loss, many people could conceivably benefit.

- The test of MIT's effectiveness would seem more credible and practical in a real-world environment than in a laboratory.

- I felt I could be successful in recruiting participants for the study since I had worked for many years in corporate America and related well to businesspeople.

My initial motivation, then, was to test and hopefully demonstrate the effectiveness of MIT in promoting reemployment for businesspeople who had been laid off.

I later learned that exiting employees often moved through the stages of grief most commonly experienced after the loss of a loved one: shock and denial, fear and anxiety, anger, bargaining, depression, and finally acceptance. In the case of the unemployed, researchers call it "job-loss grief." If you have lost your job, you may be familiar with some or all of these grieving stages. You should understand that your feelings are normal, and that this book will show you how to manage and move through them quickly by using the MIT career-transition program I created. It has proven to be quick and easy to use and has helped many exiting employees recover and get back to work fast. The entire program can be completed in just six daily sessions of about twenty minutes each.

Where We're Going

The Job-Loss Recovery Guide is divided into three parts. Part 1 lays the foundation by describing the symptoms and stages of grief that may accompany your job loss and explaining the MIT that will help you recover. It also provides the structure of the Job-Loss Recovery Program.

You'll get a good understanding of the MIT that supports this program, what it is, what it can do for you, and its program components, which I call scenarios because each is a scripted experience. I describe the program's organizational structure, which includes the six MIT sessions mentioned.

Part 2 takes you step-by-step through Sessions 1, 2, and 3, in which you will resolve the loss, boost your self-esteem, and improve your job-search motivation and performance. I will guide you through each session.

Part 3 guides you through Sessions 4, 5, and 6, in which you will increase your self-confidence and further enhance your job-search competence.

The Job-Loss Recovery Guide will teach you how to break through the barriers that may impede success and how to create a new vision for your life. In short, you can discover in these pages the tools and resources to find success within yourself. You'll not only achieve reemployment success, but I believe you'll want to use these tools to improve your life every day.

Changing Loyalties and New Identities

You are not alone. Millions of employee layoffs have resulted from the corporate trend to restructure, downsize, and merge, bringing about enormous and far-reaching casualties. More jobs were lost in just one year (1998) than in the preceding *decade*. And the trend continues as the unthinkable happens: national corporations file for bankruptcy. It's not surprising that we live in an age of anxiety about mergers, layoffs, and the shrinking value of shareholder equities.

The U.S. economy fell into its worst hiring slump in almost twenty years in early 2003, according to an article in the February 6 *New York Times*. As of February 2003, almost 1.9 million people looking for work had been unemployed for at least six months, triple the number of those in 2001. About one million people appear to have dropped out of the work force between the summer of 2002 and February 2003, suggesting that the pain of joblessness has worsened (Leonhardt 2003).

This book will help you heal the pain and significantly decrease your landing time. David Noer, Vice President for Training and Education at the Center for Creative Leadership, outlines a paradigm shift in his book addressed to those people remaining in organizations after downsizing has occurred. In *Healing the Wounds: Overcoming the Trauma of Layoffs and Revitalizing Downsized Organizations* (1995), Noer says that organizations that used to see employees as long-term assets to be developed, now see them as short-term costs to be reduced. He also notes that employees have, traditionally, obtained their sense of identity and self-esteem from the organization. And he recommends that clients use guided imagery to personally explore work-related issues.

In light of this organizational shift, if you want to develop a more authentic and lasting sense of identity and self-esteem, you must stop defining yourself in relation to your business organization. Instead, connect with a personal core purpose, awaken your spirit, gain control over your life, and engage in work that reflects your ideal self. If you believe this is out of reach for you, now is a good time to consider stretching that belief. I'm convinced that you can achieve each of these goals using the MIT program and the techniques I share with you in *The Job-Loss Recovery Guide*.

Transforming Trauma to Triumph: How Science Supports This Book

Many people have asked me about the Job-Loss Recovery Program's underlying study, so I will give you a brief summary. If you'd like to read the published academic article in its entirety, it is referenced at the end of this book under L. M. Joseph and M. A. Greenberg.

Fifty-two professional men and women who had been laid off—primarily managers and executives—volunteered for the study. The overall objective was to compare the effectiveness of a career-transition program to a placebo control protocol in promoting reemployment. Most of us think of a sugar pill when we hear or see the word "placebo," but, in this case, placebo refers to the test condition that participants incorrectly believe is the effective condition being tested.

In this study, for example, participants were randomly assigned to two groups. Participants in each group received six sessions of a twenty-minute imagery protocol designed to make them believe it would facilitate their job search. But only one group received the career-transition program imagery.

Participants in the career-transition program group listened to a recording of my voice reading an MIT script designed to help them achieve closure, improve motivation and job-search competence, and increase confidence. Participants in the placebo control group followed written instructions to sit silently while visualizing themselves executing current job-search plans for half of each twenty-minute session; and, for the remaining half, visualizing future job-search plans.

The result of the study was astonishing: two months after their sessions, *five times* more participants in the career-transition program group had begun full-time, permanent work than had the placebo control group participants. It's unusual in academic research to find such a large difference between groups. As an added bonus to the study results, participants who accepted jobs within two months did not suffer a decrease in salary. The program worked well and it worked fast, as I'd hoped. The graph below shows the results after two months and four months.

Reemployment

Participants in the study ranged in age from twenty-nine to sixty-four, with an average age of forty-seven, and almost two-thirds were back to work in two months or less, following the program.

You can be, too.

I wrote this book for independent use. All MIT scripts are included to either read or record for your own playback. If, however, you prefer to use professionally recorded Job-Loss Recovery Program scripts, see the Author's Note in the back of this book for contact information. You may want to designate a specific notebook or journal as your Job-Loss Recovery Journal. It will be useful to track your progress and to make notes as you complete the suggested exercises.

PART 1

Laying the Foundation: What This Program Will Do for You

CHAPTER 1

Job Loss: A Traumatic Event

People are like stained-glass windows. They sparkle and shine when the sun is out, but when darkness sets in, their true beauty is revealed only if there is a light from within.

—Elisabeth Kubler-Ross

Standing in his boss's office, forty-five-year-old Paul felt as if he'd just been kicked in the stomach. He'd been laid off after ten years of loyal service. He felt his very life had been yanked from him.

How would his family survive? He received some company severance pay and had put aside a little money for emergencies. But it wouldn't last long, and he feared for their future.

In the ensuing weeks, Paul had trouble sleeping and concentrating and often felt depressed. He blamed himself for having lost his job. He wondered if he had worked harder and for longer hours, whether he'd have been let go. But deep down he knew he'd been a good worker. He felt humiliated, abandoned, and betrayed by his company.

Paul's reaction is common, and his fear and anxiety are justified. Studies show, at his age, finding another job may take over five months in a "normal" economic environment.

Typically, severance pay is one week's salary per year of service. This means the average manager with five years' tenure would receive only five weeks' salary on termination. Even Paul's ten weeks' severance pay clearly won't support a five-month job search. And surveys indicate that when managers and professionals are rehired after being laid off, they often earn 20 to 30 percent less than in their previous positions.

Psychologists recognize job loss as one of life's most traumatic experiences. It's a stressful, life-changing event—one that can lead to negative mental and physical health consequences and jeopardize financial security and family relationships.

Soon after the terrorist attacks of September 11, 2001, Georgia Witkin, Ph.D., Assistant Clinical Professor of Psychiatry and Director of the Stress Program at the Mount Sinai School of Medicine in New York City, gave a stress-relief workshop to 1500 employees of the Syosset, Long Island, School District. Many of the employees were in shock and grieving for their lost loved ones and neighbors while simultaneously trying to help their students overcome fear and anger.

The group was asked to write down their most stressful experience before the terrorist attacks. Then they were asked to rate that experience on a scale of one (lowest stress) to ten (highest stress), and then to rate their stress from the terrorist attacks on the same scale. To the surprise of Dr. Witkin and the researchers at the Stress Program, although the horrible terrorist trauma received relevantly high stress ratings, the personal traumas and losses got even higher stress ratings. Dr. Witkin concluded that, clearly, no disaster is small if the loss is personal.

Therefore, please do not minimize the personal impact of your job loss. It is absolutely normal for you and your family to feel a great deal of stress.

You may want to pause for a moment to rate your job-loss stress on a scale of one to ten. What number came to mind? As a comparison, the stress rating for the September eleventh disaster averaged 7.8 stress points.

The loss of your job requires coping efforts. In this context, "coping" means the process of managing the stressful situation and the emotions that situation brings up. How you perceive, appraise, and cope with the loss will then largely determine how quickly you recover. Your appraisal will determine why and to what degree a situation is stressful.

There is a widely held myth that our thoughts are a result of our feelings. You would first feel frightened, for instance, and then mentally appraise the situation as frightening. In truth, it most often works in reverse; that is, you first think the situation is frightening, and then you feel frightened. Accordingly, if you change your thoughts about the situation, your feelings will also change.

The Job-Loss Recovery Program in this book will help you improve your coping skills and shift your thoughts, assisting you to appraise your job-loss situation more rationally and productively as a challenge rather than a threat.

John F. Kennedy once said, "When written in Chinese, the word 'crisis' is composed of two characters—one represents danger and the other represents opportunity." I hope you'll recognize the hidden opportunity in your current situation. Though it may not seem like it at the moment, your experience of it is really a matter of perspective.

Along with helping you to develop your inner management skills, this tested and proven program is designed to put you back in control of your career, so when you take the actions necessary to get back to work, you'll be far more successful, far more quickly.

Stages and Symptoms of Job-Loss Grief

If you are a victim of corporate downsizing, merging, or restructuring, understand that it's normal for you to have symptoms and emotions such as the following:

- Shame
- Fear
- Anxiety
- Sense of abandonment and betrayal
- Anger
- Guilt
- Loss of self-esteem
- Loss of confidence
- Sadness
- Depression
- Feelings of failure
- Loneliness
- Irritability
- Loss of appetite
- Trouble sleeping
- Bad dreams

The list is long and may seem intimidating. In fact, this section about the stages and symptoms of job-loss grief may feel a little discouraging. Yet, the first step on the path of healing is to recognize and own what you're feeling. Only then can you resolve those feelings and begin to take back control of your life.

Research tells us that the strongest predictors of negative reactions to job loss are financial distress and attachment to the previous job. In other words, the more stress you feel over meeting financial demands or the more involved you were in your last job, the more distressed you are likely to feel. Your initial reaction may be to hold back any heavy emotions and get on with your job search.

Yet, by stuffing your uncomfortable thoughts and feelings, you can put yourself at greater risk for negative results, including illness. At the very least, this inhibition can reduce your ability to mentally work through many aspects of the stressful event, which results in your distressing thoughts and feelings just getting worse.

So you can see how denying, avoiding, or feeling guilty about your feelings is really counterproductive to healing—and to conducting a successful job search. You simply need to take the time to grieve.

Many authorities, including the late, renowned authority on death and dying, Elisabeth Kubler-Ross, explain unemployment as a trauma that induces reactions similar to the loss of a loved one or to facing terminal illness, an experience that requires a period of grieving. Dr. Kubler-Ross recognized and formulated the stages of grieving most people experience after the loss of a loved one (1997).

- Shock and denial

- Fear and anxiety

- Anger

- Bargaining

- Depression

- Acceptance

The stages have been widely documented to apply to job loss, as well. Losing a job can initiate some or all of these stages, and they can be experienced in any order.

In *Career Bounce-Back* (1998), J. Damian Birkel has modified these stages to more accurately reflect the job-loss grief process he calls the "emotional wave" (or "e-wave," for short). According to the e-wave model, when you hear you've been terminated, you are thrown into an ocean of emotional waves.

As you begin the climb up one wave, you are first in the shock and denial stage, followed by the fear and anxiety stage. As you move up the crest of the wave, you pass through the stages of anger, bargaining, depression, and finally the trough of the wave and what Birkel calls "temporary acceptance." It's temporary because, unlike Kubler-Ross's more permanent acceptance stage following the death of a loved one, you will cycle through many more waves before you learn to confront and manage your e-wave emotions. At that point, you can safely reach the shore.

Remember though, you may not even experience all of the stages. On the other hand, you may cycle through some of the stages more than once. Let's take a closer look at one client's journey through each of the stages. You may recognize your own feelings in his story.

Richard, a thirty-eight-year-old accountant and department manager, experienced his layoff notification a little differently than Paul. When he first heard about his job termination, he thought, "This can't be happening to me. It happens to other people, not me. They'll find out they made a mistake and call me back."

Richard had experienced the shock and denial stage. Numbness set in.

Shock and numbness are the body-mind's ways of allowing us to function on automatic pilot—without interference from distressing emotions—for a few hours after any traumatic event. Nothing seems real, and you feel detached. In fact, you may not feel the full impact of your job loss for days or even weeks.

When Richard broke the news to his family, he sensed the fear they tried to hide behind a stoic front. He then began to realize the reality of his situation and moved into the fear and anxiety stage, where he stayed for several weeks. Since he had lost control of his career, he began to lose confidence in himself. His thoughts raced from, "I haven't had to look for a job in years," to "What if no employer wants me?" on to "I could lose everything."

Richard felt abandoned and betrayed by his company because so much that he valued had been taken away from him. He felt terribly vulnerable.

Panic emerged and, as he feared the worst, small issues began to take on overwhelming importance. At this point, he could easily have become immobilized.

Richard felt he'd been a loyal, hard-working employee and deserved better than a pink slip. He'd been dealt a serious blow that he experienced as an injustice. But, unfortunately, he hadn't allowed himself the anger that was his right. Rather than experience the anger stage, he unconsciously turned his wrath inward and instead became depressed, skipping right over the bargaining stage. He began thinking he deserved to lose his job, that it was his fault, and that he should have known enough to circulate his resume long before his layoff.

I'd like you to bear in mind that when you direct anger at yourself (such as Richard did when he blamed himself for being laid off), you set up a downward-spiral pattern that can lead to depression and immobility—not what you need to move forward productively.

Four months into his job search, with severance pay long gone and little savings left, Richard began bargaining with God: "If you help me find a job, I'll never take it for granted again."

Richard's wife sensed his desperation and felt helpless. She then saw an article about my career-transition program and encouraged him to contact me. He did.

Once Richard managed to resolve his feelings and to evaluate his situation more positively, he felt closure on his past job and progressed to the acceptance stage. That important step paved the way for him to clearly and aggressively focus on getting the job he wanted. Soon after he completed the program, he received and accepted a good offer from a company he had targeted. But he had to come to terms with his feelings—to let himself grieve—before he could put his energy toward his search.

Goals for a Quick Recovery

A key goal of the Job-Loss Recovery Program, then, is to help you move quickly through the stages of grieving to a once-and-for-all acceptance with closure. But other important goals follow that one. For example, you might very well have damaged confidence and self-esteem, as well as other anxiety-producing feelings related to gaining reemployment. These issues also need to be addressed.

Thus, this program was designed to help you achieve each of the following goals for a quick recovery:

··· Learn to relax and manage your stress.

··· Process and resolve any distressing emotional reactions.

··→ Boost your confidence and self-esteem.

··→ Improve job-search competence.

··→ Take control of your future.

··→ Renew and maintain hope.

··→ Land the job of your choice.

The first goal is to manage your stress by learning to relax. You will be guided through an exercise to reduce external distractions, slow your breathing, and decrease muscle tension, which will result in greater calm and more-focused thinking. All of your program sessions will be preceded by this relaxation exercise and will be more effective as a result.

When you leave negative feelings unexpressed and unprocessed, you may unintentionally block your success in the job search. In fact, research has shown emotional expression to be effective in promoting reemployment. Therefore, the second goal is to resolve any distressing feelings and fully accept the employment termination. This will enhance your motivation and promote a successful job search as you apply this new, positive attitude to organizing, assimilating, and finding meaning in the event. In other words, you will then reach closure on that part of your past.

In one layoff study, exit interviews were taped with forty-seven exiting employees (LaFarge 1994). All felt ambivalent about leaving their companies and colleagues. They vacillated between wanting to stay while feeling righteous anger toward the organization for terminating them and wanting to leave the job and company behind. They described separation grief as painful. Yet, they had mixed feelings about letting go of the grief because it was their last connection with the company. Many also fluctuated between trying to justify the corporate actions and condemning those same hurtful actions.

Interestingly—and this may apply to you—most were unaware of their ambivalence. The more immediate needs of finding a new job and explaining things to friends and family were given precedence over exploring their own emotions. The researchers concluded that this failure to recognize and explore mixed feelings contributed to their difficulty in accepting and moving on and could, in addition, contribute to a delayed emotional investment in a new organization.

The displaced workers felt uncomfortable emotions yet, at the same time, recognized the opportunities for growth. Coping with these

---

EXPRESSING EMOTIONS SAFELY
PROMOTES REEMPLOYMENT.

---

vacillating feelings that resulted in anxiety became one of the most difficult tasks they faced in resolving their trauma.

Many of the former employees in the same investigation also fluctuated between feelings of competence and powerlessness. They wanted to believe in their competence, and cited many examples to support this belief, while, at the same time, the layoff had made many of them feel unsure of themselves and of their ability to function effectively.

Another interesting study tested the effects of written emotional expression—also called "emotional disclosure"—on obtaining reemployment success. Spera, Buhrfeind, and Pennebaker (1994) conducted the study with sixty-three professional participants (mostly engineers). The group's average age was fifty-four and they had been with their former employer an average of twenty years. All were recruited at an outplacement firm following a large-scale layoff from their company.

Participants were assigned to either a disclosive writing group, a control writing group, or a nonwriting control group. The disclosive writing group wrote about their thoughts and feelings regarding their termination for twenty minutes a day, for five days. The control writing group wrote about nontraumatic topics and the nonwriting control group did not write at all.

Three months after the writing week, 25 percent of the participants in the disclosive writing group were employed, none of the writing control participants had success, and 9 percent of the nonwriting control participants had jobs. Thus, those who wrote about the trauma of losing their jobs were significantly more likely to find reemployment in the months following the study than those who did not.

The Job-Loss Recovery Program will guide you safely through an emotional-expression scenario that will occur in your mind rather than in writing. In addition, you'll be able to do the exercise in a way that's designed to promote resolution and closure. You'll learn more about that process in chapter 5.

Two other important goals for a quick recovery are to regain confidence through self-esteem and to improve job-search competence. The entire program is designed to boost your confidence, but nowhere will you benefit more than in the mental-rehearsal scenario where you will practice your interviewing skills. Mentally rehearsing job interviews will also improve your job-search performance. I explain mental rehearsal and its benefits in chapter 7.

Renewed self-esteem can provide a significant advantage in an interview, affecting how aggressively and persuasively you sell your job skills. In addition, high self-esteem is a quality sought after by most employers. In fact, many researchers have found a strong relationship between career success and positive self-esteem.

ACCEPTING THE LOSS, MAINTAINING A
POSITIVE ATTITUDE, AND FEELING IN
CONTROL PROMOTE FASTER REEMPLOYMENT.

If you don't currently have the skills to conduct an effective job search and do not receive outplacement services, there are quite a number of resources that can help you out. For example, many books are available to help improve your skills in resume and letter writing, interviewing, and negotiating job offers.

The fifth goal of the Job-Loss Recovery Program is to help you take control of your future. People's inability to prevent the loss of their job is typically felt as a loss of personal control, which conflicts with the wish we all have for power and mastery. You will be reminded throughout this book that you are in total control of your thoughts, feelings, and behaviors. As you move through the program, accepting the loss, planning the future, and rehearsing success, your sense of control and emotional mastery will develop and expand.

The sixth goal for a quick recovery is for you to maintain hope throughout the job search. Positive beliefs are a key forerunner to an effective search for reemployment. This program will help you to see job loss as a challenge to overcome, and as an experience from which you can learn and grow.

When you achieve the six goals above, the seventh—landing the job of your choice—should happen naturally. When you can honestly put the past behind, rebuild your confidence and self-esteem, perform competently in job-search activities, feel in control of your life, and think optimistically, you *will* find positive reemployment.

One more thing: take time to laugh. Laughter blocks anxiety and fear by releasing the body's stress-reducing biochemicals.

How This Book Will Help You

Your journey of growth has begun, and the first step along the path is opening this book. In these pages you will learn to quickly and easily take control of your career despite the emotional setback of job loss. You will empower yourself with new tools to heal wounds, to create success and happiness, and even to find meaning and purpose.

Does this sound miraculous? Maybe it does, depending on your perspective. The *Random House Webster's College Dictionary* (2001) defines a miracle as an event that surpasses known human powers or natural forces. The operative word is "known." Today, scientists know more about human potential than just a few years ago. They better understand how the mind and body work—and how they work together. What we previously thought was impossible now seems very possible.

> ## YOU WILL LEARN TO QUICKLY RESOLVE DISTRESSING EMOTIONS AND TAKE CONTROL OF YOUR CAREER.

I challenge you to put aside skepticism for the moment. Read this book and earnestly implement the program. After all, it's not that much of a sacrifice—the entire program can be completed in just six daily sessions of about twenty minutes each.

Here are some tips that will help you make the most of this book.

- Make the Job-Loss Recovery Program an integral part of your job search. Reserve a time for the sessions now in your daily planner.

- Complete the questionnaires honestly so you can track your emotional progress as you advance through the program.

- Actively engage in the additional exercises provided to improve your self-understanding and MIT skills. As your skills improve, your sessions will have an increasingly positive impact on your job search.

I will lead you through the entire process, as you resolve your most difficult feelings and improve job-search performance.

Level of Distress Questionnaire

Please take a few minutes right now to complete the following Level of Distress Questionnaire. Don't put it off. It will help you identify the symptoms of stress that may interfere with your success. In an effort to cope with uncomfortable feelings, you may be suppressing them or pushing them aside, unaware of their potential impact on your job search.

I will be asking you to complete the questionnaire now, after your third program session, and when you have completed the sixth session. This repetition will enable you to track your return to emotional health, watching your distress score drop lower and lower. The final question reflects your sense of control over job loss. As you begin to feel more in control of your situation, your score will drop on that single statement as well.

The significance of your initial total score is relative. It simply reflects your level of distress and will be used only for comparison with your later scores as you advance through the program. There are no good or bad scores. You already know you're feeling stressed, or you wouldn't be reading this book. This questionnaire will help you to see your progress.

As stress-relief expert Dr. Witkin (2002) puts it, "We're built for emotional survival." You know you will get through this challenge. Make the choice to grow wiser, stronger, and more resilient as a result of it.

In chapter 2, I will explain MIT in more detail: how it's used today in several arenas, what it can do for you, and how this program can help you get back to work fast.

Level of Distress Questionnaire

The statements listed below refer to your inner feelings in regard to your job loss. Using the following scale from 1 to 10, insert the number that most closely reflects your current feelings and state of mind.

1	2	3	4	5	6	7	8	9	10
Never		*Sometimes*			*Frequently*			*Most of the Time*	

____ I have trouble focusing on what I am doing.

____ I feel anxious.

____ I feel frustrated.

____ I have waves of distressing feelings.

____ I am reminded of my job loss often.

____ I try to ignore my feelings about my job loss.

____ I feel depressed.

____ I have trouble staying motivated.

____ I feel angry and/or resentful.

____ I have trouble sleeping because I keep thinking about my job loss.

____ I feel fearful.

____ Any reminder brings back stressful feelings.

____ I have troubling dreams about my job loss.

For this final statement, use a 1 to 10 scale but, this time, 1 indicates *Strongly Disagree* and 10 means *Strongly Agree*. Insert the number that most closely reflects your current belief, as is relevant to your job loss.

____ Little can be done to change my job-related problems.

____ **Total your score here.**

This score represents your current level of distress about your job loss and is for future comparison purposes only.

CHAPTER 2

Bounce Back with Mental Image Technology

A mind is like a parachute. It has to be open in order to work.

—Bumper sticker

What Is Mental Image Technology?

Let's first clarify terminology. There are books and seminars on the subject of "mental imagery," others on "visualization" or "creative visualization," even others on "guided imagery." It's enough to confuse anyone.

Imagery and visualization are similarly defined in *Random House Webster's College Dictionary* (2001) as "mental images" or "a mental picture," and the two terms are often used interchangeably. Because of the potential confusion created by having several terms refer to the same basic technology, I use the term mental image technology or MIT to encompass all of them.

Simply put, MIT is a thought process that directs and focuses the imagination to create an experience in the mind. It involves the body, the emotions, and all five senses: sight, sound, smell, taste, and touch.

MIT CREATES AN IMAGINARY EXPERIENCE
WITH FAR-REACHING RESULTS.

Experiencing the imagery through all five senses enhances the power and depth of your experience.

The subconscious understands images more clearly than words. Thus, imagery is considered the dominant "language" of the subconscious. Imagery also acts as a bridge between the conscious and subconscious. By consciously choosing the images you hold in your mind, you can communicate with your subconscious—the gatekeeper to your deepest motivations and emotional experiences.

When you add sensory elements to the images, your subconscious does not recognize the difference between imagination—mental imagery experiences—and reality. A good illustration of this is the story a client of mine named Joan once told me about a particularly stressful job interview. The interview room was small and smelled of stale cigarette smoke. The temperature was uncomfortably warm, and Joan felt the interviewer's questions were intended to put undue pressure on her. She felt anxious and repulsed. After a while, Joan became nauseated and left the interview.

As she related the story's details to me, Joan began to feel nauseated, as she had during the interview. I wasn't surprised. As she told the story, she relived the experience in her mind, as if she could actually hear the interviewer, feel the stuffy room, and smell the stale cigarette smoke. Her subconscious accepted the imagined experience as real, and reacted as it had during the actual experience—with nausea.

Imagined experiences can also produce changes in blood pressure, brain waves, and other bodily functions ruled by the autonomic nervous system, which is normally beyond conscious control. Because it makes use of imagery and senses, the impact of MIT on both your body and your mind can be considerable.

In this book, you'll learn to use imagery and imagined experiences positively. You'll become more aware of your thoughts and feelings and will learn to manage and direct them to your advantage.

The brain has two hemispheres that process thoughts in different ways. With the left hemisphere, we think in terms of words and logic, and with the right hemisphere, in terms of images, sounds, and feelings.

The two hemispheres also process information differently. The left brain processes sequentially (one bit of information at a time), while the right brain processes simultaneously (more than one bit of information at the same time) and has the ability to grasp the big picture. A right-brain perspective may allow you to develop creative solutions to job-search issues and is invaluable in the healing process. MIT engages both left- and right-brain activity.

I am sometimes asked if MIT is like positive thinking. Norman Vincent Peale, author of *The Power of Positive Thinking* (1996) and *Positive Imaging: The Powerful Way to Change Your Life* (1982), wrote in the latter that "Imaging is positive thinking carried one step further. So powerful is the imaging effect on thought and performance that a long-held visualization of an objective or goal can become determinative."

LEARN TO DIRECT YOUR IMAGINATION
TO YOUR ADVANTAGE.

Belleruth Naparstek, psychotherapist and author of *Staying Well with Guided Imagery* (1994), would agree. She introduced three operating principles for guided imagery that provide us with important insights into the power of MIT. First, the body does not discriminate between the mind's sensory images and actual reality. Thus, the body's systems may react to sensory images that are "only in the mind" as if they were manifested in the physical reality. When you use all five senses in a mental imagery experience, you ensure that the subconscious will participate as if the experience were actually occurring in your outer reality.

Naparstek's second operating principle states that we become capable of more swift and intense healing, growth, learning, and change when we are in an altered state—that is, a state of relaxed focus. This is largely because when we are in a state of relaxation, distractions and mental chatter seem to dissolve, and we have more direct access to our subconscious minds. (These effects are the reason you will begin each of your program sessions with a relaxation exercise.)

Finally, she asserts that guided imagery gives us a greater sense of control and mastery over what is happening to us, which promotes enhancement of both our self-esteem and our performance. I found this to be true in my job-loss study. Once the sessions were completed, participants reported increased feelings of control over their employment situation.

How MIT Is Used Today

Mark Victor Hansen and Jack Canfield are cocreators of the widely successful *Chicken Soup for the Soul* book series, selected stories that epitomize goal achievement and success. From their first self-published book they created a multi-million-dollar enterprise of book spinoffs and related products. Hansen noted how the routine use of visualization techniques—with emotion and all the senses involved—played a great part in his success.

You have probably heard the term "mind-body connection." It refers to how thoughts and feelings can impact the body and vice versa. Psychologists have long known about the reciprocal relationship between the mind and the emotions. In other words, what you think affects how you feel, and how you feel affects what you think.

In addition, considerable research has revealed how thoughts and feelings also directly affect the health and performance of the body. In her book *Molecules of Emotion* (1997), brain scientist Candace Pert, Ph.D., writes that visualization can increase the blood flow into a selected part of the body and thereby increase the availability of oxygen and nutrients to carry away toxins and nourish the cells. In a wide range of studies, mental imagery has been found to significantly impact health.

Use of imagery techniques is also linked to improved performance among athletes. It's widely known that competitive sports have become as much a mental game as a physical one, and all Olympic athletes (as well as the most successful professional athletes) now practice some form of mental imagery training to increase confidence and peak performance. In this book you will learn similar techniques to increase your confidence and improve your interview performance.

In his book *Mental Training for Peak Performance* (1996), Steven Ungerleider, Ph.D., a member of the U.S. Olympic Committee Sports Psychology Registry, recounts the personal experiences of athletes who have used mental imagery training to aid in achieving their great successes. He includes strategies used by

- ··· Janet Evans, four-time gold-medal Olympic swimmer

- ··· Mark Plaatjes, 1993 world marathon winner

- ··· Mike Pigg, number-two ranked triathlete in the world

- ··· Chuck Hogan, Johnny Miller, and Ray Floyd, professional golfers

According to Ungerleider, "The appeal of mental-imagery techniques is that we know they work. Not only does research show that imagery works, but numerous athletes swear by it" (33).

Jack Nicklaus, one of the most successful golfers of all time, has said that a full 50 percent of his game is psychological. For decades he has used an elaborate visualization process that he calls "going to the movies." According to Nicklaus (1998), before every shot he sees a color movie in his head. First, he sees the ball where he wants it to finish. Then the scene changes and he envisions the ball going there—its path, trajectory, and behavior on landing. Finally, he sees himself making the kind of swing that will turn the first two images into reality.

Arnold Schwarzenegger was also a pioneer in using visualization techniques as he worked to shape his body. His workouts were always preceded by visualizations in which he pictured the results he wanted, such as imagining his biceps as mountains.

Michael Jordan, the great Chicago Bulls basketball player and successful business entrepreneur, said he has long used visualization techniques daily to plan every step of upcoming games and ensure smooth-running business activities.

Neurolinguistic programming, known as NLP, uses imagery to reprogram the brain in order to achieve selected goals and outcomes. Richard Bandler and John Grinder formulated NLP after observing and modeling the therapeutic techniques of some of the most successful psychotherapists and hypnotherapists, among them Fritz Perls and Milton Erikson. Motivational guru Tony Robbins popularized NLP as a tool for personal growth and empowerment.

Imagery is being used today even in the workplace. David Noer, Vice President for Training and Education at the Center for Creative Leadership, uses guided imagery to explore issues and goals with many Fortune 500 executives.

What MIT Can Do for You

So often, well-meaning parents teach their children to suppress or otherwise deny their anger and pain rather than helping them to more effectively manage it. Many people have no idea how to even begin taking charge of anger, other than to pretend they simply don't have it.

The ability to manage emotions is now called "emotional intelligence," and certain cutting-edge schools are including it in the curriculum. It's about time. For too long now our cultural norms have implied that more evolved or enlightened humans do not experience the heavier emotions such as anger and hurt.

In reality, even enlightened spiritual masters feel the full range of human emotions. Thich Nhat Hanh, a Vietnamese monk in the Zen tradition, was nominated for the Nobel Peace Prize in 1967 for his tireless work for peace during the Vietnam War. He has since become internationally known for his teaching and writing on mindfulness. The book *From the Ashes* (Walsh and Beliefnet 2001) contains interviews with respected world leaders. In it, regarding the impact of September 11, 2001, Hanh recounts, "I understand the suffering of those who have lost beloved ones in this tragedy. . . . When we learned of the bombing of the Bentra village in Vietnam, where 300,000 homes were destroyed, and the pilots told journalists they had destroyed the village in order to save it, I was shocked, and [racked] with anger and grief. We practiced walking calmly and gently on the Earth to bring back our calm mind and peaceful heart" (97).

The masters have learned to recognize, feel intensely, and release heavy emotions so quickly that it *appears* as though they do not feel them. In other words, one might say they dive deeply and intensely into the emotion, move through it with understanding and forgiveness, and leap back out again. It's a skill all of us can learn.

I have used hundreds of mental imagery techniques for countless purposes in my own life over a period of many years. In upcoming pages, I share some of my own techniques as well as other methods to help you resolve your heavy emotions and create the future you want.

Make an Ally of Your Subconscious Mind

Your subconscious mind—where many undesirable emotional experiences get suppressed—can become a helpful ally in your healing process. It is capable of releasing the painful emotions and limiting beliefs that hold you back and replacing them with the positive feelings and new beliefs of your choice that can move you forward.

For example, I once held the belief that life was a struggle, that I couldn't achieve what I wanted without struggling for it. In fact, that was often the case—I did struggle for success. You might think my belief formed as a result of having experienced life as a struggle, but it's actually the other way around. I first acquired the belief,

> YOUR SUBCONSCIOUS CAN BECOME YOUR ALLY.

role-modeled by my hard-working parents, and then my life experiences developed to conform to the belief.

When I became aware that I might be unconsciously attracting events and circumstances into my life that confirmed my belief in struggle, I used mental imagery techniques to quickly change it to "Anything I desire comes to me with ease." Changing a long-held belief can be as simple as making a conscious choice. At other times, it may not be quite that easy. In chapter 9, I'll discuss more about beliefs and provide exercises for you to change those that no longer serve you well.

The program described in this book will make an ally of your subconscious, allowing you to make the shifts in thinking and feeling you'll need to get back to work fast.

Imagery techniques have been used for thousands of years in many cultures and traditions. If you're interested in the history of mental imagery, I especially like Patrick Fanning's *Visualization for Change* (1994) and *Guided Imagery for Self-Healing* (2000) by Martin Rossman, M.D. Both books provide a historical framework and describe many guided imagery techniques for improving emotional and physical health. Dr. Rossman also incorporates the latest research.

How Confident Are You Right Now?

Self-confidence is, of course, an important attribute for you to project to prospective employers. Unfortunately, losing your job may have undermined your confidence in yourself and your abilities.

Because this program is so easy to implement, you might tend to minimize its benefits. To track your increasing confidence level through the MIT program, I created the Level of Confidence Questionnaire. As with the Level of Distress Questionnaire, there are no right or wrong answers. The score is for your use only, to compare with your later score.

The questionnaire follows and will appear again in chapter 8, after you complete the final session. That way, you'll be able to compare scores, seeing how far you've come.

So please take a few minutes to rate the questions with thought and honesty. Do it now.

Level of Confidence Questionnaire

Using the following scale from 1 to 10, insert the number that most closely reflects your confidence in your ability to perform that task.

1	2	3	4	5	6	7	8	9	10

Not Confident   *Moderately Confident*   *Highly Confident*

I can

_____ manage the demands created by my job loss.

_____ use my social network to obtain job leads.

_____ do what it takes to schedule job interviews.

_____ perform successfully in a job interview.

_____ manage my emotions while unemployed.

_____ see my job loss in a more positive light.

_____ learn something from my job-loss experience.

_____ concentrate my thoughts and efforts on my job search.

_____ **Total your score here.**

This score represents your current level of confidence related to your job loss and is for comparison purposes only.

The Three Levels of an MIT Experience

You may experience your MIT program sessions on any or all of three emotional levels, depending on your intention and goals.

- ··· Relaxation and stress-relief

- ··· Closure and success

- ··· Wisdom and purpose

The first level promotes relaxation and stress reduction. Each of your sessions begins with a relaxation exercise designed to facilitate a deeper and more meaningful experience. So, at the very least, if you walk through the program without engaging much feeling, you will still benefit by relaxing and reducing your anxiety.

When you participate in the sessions with focused intention and concentration—believing it can work for you and allowing your feelings to surface—the emotional closure and successful job search you seek can take place quickly. Skepticism is healthy; however, while you are engaged in sessions, leave it aside. You will achieve better results if you fully convince yourself of the program's great benefit to you.

If you also seek new meaning and purpose in your life, you may want to use some of the MIT techniques to access an even deeper connection with inner wisdom and creativity and to explore any number of issues in your life. I hope you choose this deeper level, which will uncover a well of inner resources with which you can confidently face a fast-changing, challenging world and reach your greatest potential.

The Power Tools of Manifestation

If I could give you power tools to create the best year you've ever had, would that be of value to you? Well, I'm going to do just that. I call them "the power tools of manifestation," and we all use them to some degree, whether we know it consciously or not. They are

••• Desire

••• Expectation

••• Imagination

Let's take them one at a time.

Desire

Great achievements begin with *desire*. How many times have you achieved a goal without it? If you're ambivalent about reaching selected goals, achieving them may be a struggle—examples are when a person feels obliged to do something because of family pressures or when you choose a goal because it's expected of you. How committed would you be without real desire? How much effort and talent will you devote to a goal you're not certain you want? And what are the chances of achieving that goal under those circumstances, as opposed to a heartfelt goal?

How would it feel to be intensely committed to getting just the right job offer—doing work you really enjoy—within a certain time frame? Such a commitment can transform a dream into reality by promoting the behaviors you need to generate that event.

What is your greatest work-related desire right now? Stop a moment to make a note of it in your Journal. Feel it, and allow the feeling to permeate your body. Call upon that feeling of desire often as you experience the Job-Loss Recovery Program.

Expectation

Look at whether you honestly anticipate success. Scientific studies have shown that if you expect to fail, you probably *will* fail. Conversely, if you believe you will succeed, then your chances of success are greatly improved.

Brian Tracy, popular professional speaker, business authority, and author of *Create Your Own Future: How to Master the 12 Critical Factors of Unlimited Success* (2002), teaches what he calls the mental laws that govern our lives. One of these laws is that your expectations determine your attitude and attitude determines your reality. You get what you expect!

A former client told me a story about his daughter, Barbara, who was earning her undergraduate degree. A final exam was approaching in a challenging class, and Barbara's especially bright roommate, who had previously failed the exam and felt defensive, derided Barbara, saying she would never pass the exam. Barbara accepted the prediction and thought, "How can I pass if she couldn't?" She began to imagine the consequences of failing and became extremely anxious. She studied many hours for the test, but anxiety interfered with her retention and testing performance, and she failed the exam—just as she'd expected.

Barbara later met with her instructor, who was surprised at the failed exam because Barbara had always been a good student. They reviewed some of the test questions together, and Barbara got every one of them right.

What had happened? Barbara had compared herself to her roommate, believed a negative prediction, and went into the exam expecting to fail. She allowed the roommate to significantly influence her thinking, her attitude, and, therefore, her chance of success.

Expectation can affect us in other significant ways as well. Participants' expectations have been shown to impact scientific study results. In the introduction to this book, I defined placebo as a test condition that participants incorrectly believe is the effective condition being tested. Now, I will expand upon that definition, showing how the good effects people seemingly got from their placebo treatments were really a result of their expectations.

A placebo is an ineffective and harmless procedure or technique —a pill with no medication in it, in many cases. A *placebo effect* refers to the positive, measurable results study participants actually get based solely on their beliefs and expectations. In other words, the patient's, or study participant's, response stems from *belief* in the procedure or drug rather than from the procedure or drug itself.

Drug studies are classic examples. Participants are randomly assigned to one of two or three groups: one group receives pills containing the actual medicine being investigated, and a second group (the placebo control group) is given placebo pills containing only sugar. Both groups believe they are receiving the effective medicine. When a third group (the control group) is included, it gets no pills at all.

Typically, the first two groups get positive results. If the medicine is found effective, the first group, which received the actual medicine, will get a much larger positive effect. Nevertheless, the placebo control group does receive a measurable benefit. The third group, when included, typically shows no effects, since they received no pills.

The placebo result offers but one conclusion: If you believe you're getting the real thing and expect to benefit, then you will. Scientists don't know why this occurs, but they know that it does.

Thus, the second power tool, expectation, can change the course of your life. It's important to examine whether you honestly expect success or failure in both your job search and this program. Are your expectations your own or have you adopted someone else's? Expectation is such a powerful tool that we want to be sure it's working for us and not against us.

Imagination

I cannot overemphasize that if you want to consciously change, grow, and reach selected goals, your imagination is an indispensable tool. You'll use it to explore, rehearse, and integrate the desired event or circumstance.

If you've ever imagined yourself in your future—whether working to meet a deadline or spending a leisurely Sunday afternoon doing something just for yourself—you have experienced a Future Self. This imagination process has been shown in studies to enhance effort, persistence, and performance in working toward goals. Imagining a positive Future Self has also been linked to increased life satisfaction. Internally meeting your Future Self can bring you mental, emotional, and behavioral benefits.

Another rewarding use of imagination is for mental rehearsal. This use has become increasingly popular in the field of athletics, where goal achievement is paramount. Mental rehearsal can increase your sense of effectiveness and competence and can enhance emotional mastery and problem solving. Research also shows that mental rehearsal increases the perception of having control over a stressful situation, such as job loss.

Coupling mental rehearsal with desire will also help you translate thought into action by increasing your expectancy about the imagined event, such as receiving a job offer.

This subject would not be complete without a word about the underlying, critical role of intention. Intention is the use of will. Every thought, feeling, and action is motivated by an intention. Become conscious of your true intentions before choosing a path or goal. Then desire, expectation, and imagination can bring it about. Otherwise, intention can oppose or even sabotage your goal.

Fringe Benefits

When your power tools are plugged in, you may find you get more than you ask for. For instance, I never imagined being profiled in *Fortune Magazine*. My beliefs were too limiting to think a small-town girl like me could appear in one of the nation's top business publications. Nevertheless, it happened.

Many people probably thought, "Isn't she lucky?" Do you think Donald Trump is lucky? My guess is that, on some level, he knows about these power tools of manifestation. Don't you think he walked over and over again down that block in New York City where the Trump Tower now stands, passionately imagining what it would look like and how he would make it happen? Don't you think he dreamed about it at night—seeing the construction and hearing the sounds of it being built while mentally walking through the building? You bet he did. He created his own luck in business. We can't all be Donald Trumps, of course. But we can create our own luck.

YOU CAN CREATE YOUR OWN LUCK.

In my case, my deepest desire was to make the Job-Loss Recovery Program available to displaced employees everywhere. I imagined thousands of jobless people using it to achieve healing and decrease landing time. And I mentally experienced my Future Self—the person I imagined myself to be in the future—feeling the joy of that achievement.

One day, following my presentation to a business group, a woman approached to tell me how distraught she was. "I have a daughter in Los Angeles who was laid off in a high-tech downsizing. She's been out of work for seven months now and is extremely depressed. I'm at my wit's end and don't know what to do. Do you think you can help her?"

I began working with her daughter, Sarah, an ambitious, single woman in her early thirties. She had held a high-paying job in a software company and was now waitressing to make ends meet. She felt hopeless and hadn't had a good night's sleep in several months. Sarah had never used MIT before and approached it with skepticism, but she was in crisis and willing to try anything. She had several phone sessions with me and completed my MIT Job-Loss Recovery Program recording.

Since the depressed high-tech industry was not hiring, she began seeking work in the music industry—an arena that had appealed to her for many years, but in which she had no experience. Within thirty days, Sarah called me to say, "You won't believe what happened!" She had accepted an intern position—a foot in the door—with a music company. They had given her a chance. She stepped into a field she loved with no prior experience—a feat all of her friends had said was impossible. Sarah made her own luck, too.

Now, back to *Fortune Magazine*. While Sarah was still looking for work, a reporter from the magazine called to talk with her about the job market; he was writing an article on job loss. She told him about a wonderful new visualization program that was helping her and suggested he talk with me. He said he'd love to talk with me and took my phone number. When the reporter didn't call within a week, I asked Sarah for his e-mail address and composed an introductory e-mail to him. I can tell you I sweated for hours over the composition of that message, but finally I hit "Send" and was ready for action.

Within twenty minutes, his return e-mail popped into my screen. "Let's talk," it said. We set up a phone interview, and he profiled my program in the magazine.

The message I hope you take from this story is that you have to create your own luck and look for opportunities everywhere. Always ask for what you want, and then take action to get it—provided that no one is harmed. When your intention is clear, when you have strong desire and an expectation to succeed, and when you use imagination to explore and experience the desired goal, success may come faster than you expected—and in more ways than you imagined.

Thus, desire, expectation, and imagination are powerful tools you can access to help you on your journey to reemployment. There will be ample opportunities to engage each of them in this program.

Now that you've been introduced to MIT, let's take a moment to put a sample of it into practice. You may want to read through these instructions first and then close your eyes to experience the scenario with fewer distractions.

Take several deep breaths, inhaling deeply and exhaling fully. Imagine yourself holding your planner and scheduling six MIT program sessions. Despite any healthy skepticism, you want to give your best effort to this program in order to receive the most benefit. Sense yourself moving through each of the sessions even though you don't yet know their complete content. Imagine feeling more and more relaxed, letting go of your fears and worries, even enjoying the experiences. Think about how your life is already changing for the better, and how it will feel as you leave the uncomfortable past behind and move forward with new hope and positive expectations. You're taking back control of your life, and it feels good. As you move through the program, sense your confidence growing until you know in both your mind and heart that you are creating the successful future you want and deserve. New directions and exciting opportunities are developing. Belief can be a conscious choice. Make the choice now to believe and to expect that out of crisis and adversity will come success, meaning, and purpose. Now open your eyes and sit with the experience for a moment.

In the next chapter, you'll learn more about the structure of the Job-Loss Recovery Program and how to make the most of it.

CHAPTER 3

The Job-Loss
Recovery Program

Don't find fault, find a remedy.
—Henry Ford

The Program's Foundation

The foundation of this book includes a unique system of MIT that I developed for my doctoral dissertation study, a system motivated by the knowledge that traumatic losses can block us from moving forward successfully, and a quick recovery is dependent upon emotionally resolving these losses.

The Job-Loss Recovery Program uses a combination of relaxation exercises plus four imagery scenarios that you will undertake repeatedly in just six sessions.

In sessions 1, 2, and 3, you will mentally and emotionally resolve the feelings associated with the loss of your job. If you've been holding on to anything you'd like to say to a former employer, here is where you'll find resolution. I will teach you the method of express yourself in your sessions, which will help bring closure to any of your unresolved feelings. This critical first step of emotional resolution begins the process of leaving the past job behind and moving on to a new one.

THE JOB-LOSS RECOVERY PROGRAM GUIDES YOU
THROUGH SIX SCRIPTED SESSIONS TO

- RESOLVE JOB-LOSS DISTRESS
- BUILD YOUR SELF-CONFIDENCE
- IMPROVE INTERVIEW PERFORMANCE
- LAND THE JOB OF YOUR CHOICE

In these sessions, I will also mentally introduce you to your happiest, most successful Future Self. This can help you build hope and self-esteem, as well as prompt some great ideas. This simple experience will also increase your motivation and improve your performance in the job search.

In the final three sessions, you will mentally rehearse peak-performance job interviews. In addition, you will mentally create and interact with your Mentor, from whom you will feel unconditional support. This experience can help you to further develop your career dreams and access wisdom deep within you.

Overall, the scenario experiences are relaxing and positive. If this is your first exposure to MIT, don't worry about not having the skills. I will instruct and guide you through each step and you will improve with practice.

MIT Scripts and How to Use Them

The program utilizes MIT scripts, which are scenarios or narratives designed to guide you through specific mental experiences. You may also think of the scripts as instructions. The basic program scripts are divided into two modules: Module 1 and Module 2.

In addition to these two basic scripts, I've provided supplemental scripts (most of which appear in appendix B) to enhance your MIT skills and provide you with even more resources to promote reemployment success. These scripts are labeled as numbered exercises to distinguish them from the Module 1 and Module 2 program scripts in the text.

There are different ways to use the scripts. I recommend you record an audiotape of them, especially if MIT is new to you. Even with my many years of experience, I often prefer to use a recorded script. It frees me to follow along and become deeply immersed in the experience, rather than have to think about what I should do next.

If you record your own tapes, practice reading the scripts aloud very slowly before you record. Pause where indicated by "..." to allow the suggested experience to unfold. Keep a relaxed tone in your voice because you will want to listen to a calm, slow-paced voice while in session. Use your own name as you read, to reinforce the messages. Your own voice should also sound pleasant to you. If it doesn't, you might ask a family member or friend whose voice you do like to read or record the scripts for you. Consider playing soothing music while recording the Basic Relaxation Skills script. Choose whatever music makes you feel calm and peaceful. An extremely slow rhythm usually accomplishes this best. Check the sound quality early in the recording process by recording a line or two of script and then playing it back. You can then adjust the settings. This trial run can also prevent you from accidentally leaving the pause button on, a frustrating (and surprisingly common) experience after you've recorded for twenty minutes.

If your choice is to read the scripts each time instead of listening to them recorded, then read through them a couple of times prior to becoming focused and involved in the experiences. This will give you a clear understanding of the entire flow and will enable you to later keep your eyes closed as you walk through the mental scenarios. If you need prompting while in a deep state of relaxation, you can open your eyes briefly to glance at the script. It's a good idea to highlight key transition points in the script ahead of time, to help you find them quickly.

Program Structure

Each of the two modules of scripts is repeated three times, providing the total of six sessions. Again, repetition adds important impact to the experience and is critical to the program's success. Although you will use the same basic procedure for three different sessions, each one of your applied personal experiences will be unique. For example, as you execute Module 1's process of resolution and closure, you may choose to mentally express your thoughts and feelings to your former boss while in Session 1, and then to mentally express your sense of personal loss to former colleagues in Session 2.

Another example: In sessions 4, 5, and 6 (Module 2), you will mentally rehearse job interviews and then meet with an inner mentor. With each succeeding session, communications with your mentor will flow more easily. Input and feedback will become more clear. Further, you may decide each time to mentally rehearse interviews for different jobs, with different interviewers questioning you. In other words, you will follow the same basic procedure in the three sessions, but your actual experiences will be different from each other.

All sessions include the basics of relaxation and establishing an emotionally safe place plus two scenarios, organized in the following way:

Module 1: Sessions 1, 2, and 3 all include:

··• Basic Relaxation and Safe Place

··• Emotional Closure

··• Meeting Your Future Self

Module 2: Sessions 4, 5, and 6 all include:

··• Basic Relaxation and Safe Place

··• Mentally Rehearsing a Job Interview

··• Meeting Your Mentor

Don't worry about what to do and when. I will guide you through each step of the entire process. The first sessions in Module 1 begin at the end of chapter 4, and you will begin Module 2 after completing chapter 6.

Schedule no more than one session a day. This will allow enough time and space for proper mental and emotional absorption and integration of the experiences.

To receive maximum benefit from the program, it's essential to implement it as it's laid out. The scripts were designed to be experienced in the order I've presented. For example, it's important that your job-loss grief is mostly resolved and that you feel closure before moving on to Module 2's mental-rehearsal scenario, because grief and stress can block success. If you participate in a job interview while holding these blocking feelings, they will affect your attitude and performance.

I learned a valuable lesson about attitude in my first corporate sales position. When I was in my mid-twenties a pharmaceutical company hired me to promote baby formula and medications to the pediatric health-care community. On my first morning, while loading the trunk of my car with products slated for delivery to a pediatric hospital unit, I dropped a twenty-pound case of formula on my left foot, breaking three bones. After loudly articulating a few choice words, I drove to a hospital where a medic applied a cast from the knee down.

I was embarrassed and felt very angry with myself. I had so wanted to perform well in my new job and make a good impression on the clients. My mood, needless to say, had soured. The baby formula was needed, however, and I'd always tended to see the positive side of a situation, so I decided to make the best of it. I put on the sincerest smile I could muster under the circumstances and made the delivery that very day.

When I hobbled into the pediatric unit pulling behind me a luggage cart filled with formula, you'd never have known it was my first visit. Heads turned, and several nurses—including the head nurse—approached to help. They called me a real trooper for making calls on the day I broke my foot. We were soon chatting like friends.

The entire month went on in a similar way as I met all of my physician and hospital clients. What an icebreaker that broken foot was!

The decision to look for the best in my situation allowed me to take advantage of an opportunity that I might not otherwise have recognized. Rather than seeing myself as disabled in my new job, I squared my shoulders and ventured forward, reframing the situation positively. Had I approached clients while wallowing in self-pity and anger, I'm certain I wouldn't have been welcomed the way I was. For the first time, I consciously acknowledged the power of positive attitude. It was a valuable lesson.

If you're having difficulty seeing anything positive in your current situation, you may find this program will turn that around. Although the entire program can be completed in six sessions, some clients who have had to deal with more severe job-loss trauma have benefited from additional work with Module 1.

Jack is a good example. He was employed by a major shipping service corporation for twenty-five years and had relocated several times as his career progressed. The company played a significant role in his life and, as you might imagine, his layoff left him with painful broken ties. He had also experienced several traumatic work-related events during his years with the company and came to me holding strong issues about the insensitive way the corporation had laid him off. Because of the severity of his trauma, Jack reported reaching full emotional closure only after six sessions with Module 1.

Each person is unique. Let your feelings set your pace. In this way, you will achieve the greatest possible benefit from the program.

How to Make the Most of Your MIT Sessions

Whether you are new to mental image technology or have lots of experience, there are several things you can do to enhance your success with the Job-Loss Recovery Program.

- ··▪ Most people relax more completely while lying down rather than sitting up. In a sitting position, your head and neck are typically not supported, so it's more difficult to fully relax. The idea is to get as comfortable and relaxed as possible. If lying down tends to encourage falling asleep, try a semi-lying position where your head can be supported, yet you're sitting up enough to keep awake. Experiment a little during the first couple of sessions.

- ··▪ If you happen to fall asleep during sessions, you may not be getting enough sleep at night. Practicing the relaxation and imagery skills will help you learn to stay awake while in a deep state of relaxation. You might also try keeping your eyes open during sessions, focusing on a set point directly in front of you.

- ··▪ Remove your shoes and wear loose clothing. I sometimes use an eye mask to block out as much light as possible. This makes it easier to turn inward and focus more fully on the MIT scenarios.

- ··▪ Find a room where you can have privacy—perhaps your office or a bedroom—and ask family members to respect a quiet time for about twenty minutes while you are "in session."

- ··▪ If your environment is not quiet, you may want to use a fan as white noise or use headphones to block distracting sounds, whether or not you are listening to recorded scripts.

- ··▪ Have your Journal at hand so that you can make notes while remaining in a quiet, reflective state.

No Experience Necessary

If this is your first exposure to mental image technology, you needn't be concerned about your lack of experience. Most of the study's participants had no prior experience using imagery techniques, yet 62 percent of those who used MIT found jobs within two months. Had the study included the additional sessions and more in-depth information that this book has, perhaps many more would have become reemployed during that time.

Since most of the participants in the study reported they'd had no previous experience with MIT, I was curious to know their feelings about their participation in the process. Therefore, after the last session and again two months later, I asked them to write down how they felt about their study experience and to comment on the overall project. Allison's comments are representative of several.

At age forty-one and a single mother, Allison had joined a company as marketing director just two months prior to her layoff. She had sought reemployment for three months before entering the study through an outplacement firm, and she felt understandably distraught. Allison had no prior experience with MIT and was skeptical at first, but she thought it was worth a try. Following her last session, Allison wrote, "I felt relaxed and in control . . . safe and hopeful. Also, this study helped to build inner peace and confidence." Within two months, Allison settled comfortably into a new position as art director for a growing young company.

Here's what other participants had to say:

"Glad I went through this. I will try to remember the process and do it on my own in this and future events."

"Had difficulty staying focused, yet felt extremely relaxed and peaceful. My mind had a tendency to wander when I couldn't generate clear pictures."

"I feel more confident and actually think this will help make my transition from my old career to a new career. Overall, I have gained confidence that I will find my perfect job."

"I think the greatest help for me has been in demonstrating the value of guided imagery. Potential is clearly there, but I think for it to work for me, I need to start with a consistently more relaxed state and need more time."

"More in control. Greater sense of perspective. Sessions 1–3 can be used to deal with other life issues. Daily use of the session would have great therapeutic value, which is why I would like a copy of the tape."

So, even with no prior MIT experience and a very short introduction during the study, participants felt they received value from their sessions. You can, too.

You are now ready to learn the details of Module 1. I'll start by introducing you to the benefits of relaxation and your first MIT script.

PART II

The Power of Closure: Module 1

CHAPTER 4

Relax and Create a Safe Place

The cyclone derives its powers from a calm center. So does a person.

—Norman Vincent Peale

Benefits of Relaxation

You will begin each MIT program session with a relaxation exercise that includes decreasing muscle tension, slowing breathing, and visiting an imaginary safe place. In addition to reducing stress, the exercise helps you reduce bodily and environmental distractions. As a result, your physical comfort is enhanced, making it easier to focus more fully on your mental experience. Many healing traditions employ this critical first step.

Formal relaxation training is most often associated with the "progressive relaxation" introduced by Edmund Jacobson, M.D. (1938). Progressive-relaxation training involves alternately tensing and relaxing sixteen different muscle groups. Recently, researchers have found that progressive relaxation training is equally effective with or without the tensing component; thus, "passive relaxation training" was formally named by James C. Overholser (1990), and is used in this program. In other words, you will relax your muscles without first tensing them.

Relaxation through breathing is a quick and easy way to reduce stress any time, whether at work, paying bills, or running errands. Breathing is affected by your emotional condition. When we feel under stress, for example, we become short of breath. But you can control your breathing by simply becoming conscious of it and slowing it down. By calming your breathing, you'll also calm your body and mind, reducing your stress level.

To give yourself a respite from tension and stress, you'll need to breathe deeply into your diaphragm. When you watch a sleeping baby breathe while lying on its back, you'll notice the belly moving in and out. That's the natural and healthy way to breathe. Most of us have developed the habit of shallow breathing, with expansion and contraction of the chest rather than the belly. As you are guided through this program's relaxation script, consciously slow your breathing while taking deep breaths in and out, exhaling fully, and feeling your belly move in and out.

I will also be guiding you through passive relaxation of your muscle groups, focusing on each muscle group and directing it to relax and release any tension it may hold.

Try a bit of the process now. Sit with your feet on the floor or lie down. Place your attention on your feet. Feel all of the muscles in your feet and toes slowly relax and begin to feel very loose and warm. If you find it difficult to sense your feet and toes relaxing, try tensing them first and then relaxing them. This is progressive muscle relaxation, and tensing first will teach your body to recognize and relax individual muscle groups. When you've relaxed this way a few times, you may no longer have the need to tense before relaxing your muscles.

The program's Basic Relaxation Skills script also includes instructions for you to create an imaginary safe place in nature. Once there, you will drink in its calm and peace. All of your MIT scenarios will take place, or at least begin, in this safe place. This pattern will condition your mind to promptly return to the relaxed state each time you revisit. In fact, should you feel the need to destress at any time in the course of your day, you may want to take a mini mental trip to your safe place and feel anxiety melt away.

Since relaxation itself has many benefits and applications in your life, I've included a relaxation script in this chapter. It's similar to the script that appears in Module 1. Begin practicing with it now so you can receive help reducing stress right away and be able to relax more deeply when you get to the Module 1 program script in chapter 6.

Script: Basic Relaxation Skills

Find a comfortable position. . . . Gently close your eyes. Begin by focusing on your breathing—inhaling deeply . . . and exhaling fully. . . . Allow your abdomen to expand and contract as you breathe deep into your diaphragm. . . . And again . . . breathing in relaxation . . . and breathing out any tension in your body. . . . Inhale . . . exhale . . . relaxing more and more . . . becoming more calm with every breath. . . . Imagine any distracting thoughts drifting away. . . . For the moment, your mind is still . . . feeling calm and relaxed now . . . inhaling deeply . . . and exhaling.

Enjoy these few moments in peaceful relaxation. . . . Notice the heaviness as your muscles begin to relax. . . . As I count down from ten to one, allow yourself to become more and more relaxed. . . . Imagine all the anxiety flowing out of you as you relax deeper and deeper. . . . Ten, nine, eight, going deeper, seven, six, five, four, going even deeper, three, two, one. . . . Very good. . . . Allow these feelings of relaxation to spread through your body. . . . You may notice a warm, heavy feeling coming over you, a sign of deep relaxation.

Now move your attention to your feet. . . . Feel all the muscles in your feet and toes slowly relax and begin to feel very loose and warm. . . . Allow the relaxation to spread into your calves as these muscles begin to feel loose, warm, and heavy. . . . Now release any tension you feel in your knees. . . . Now feel your thigh muscles begin to relax, all the tension releasing down, out of your feet and into the earth. . . . This relaxing, peaceful feeling is a gift you're giving to yourself.

Now focus on your hips and abdomen. . . . Feel all the muscles loosening and relaxing. . . . Release any tension held there, allowing it to flow down and out of your body. . . . Now your back muscles are loosening, feeling warm. . . . Your neck and shoulders, a favorite place to hold burdens, are loosening and releasing any knots blocking you. . . . Continue to relax as you go deeper and deeper.

Move your attention to your arms, your upper and lower arms, and your hands. . . . Let go of any burdens and responsibilities. You can pick them up again later. . . . Sense your hands relaxing and warming as the tension flows out through your fingers. . . . Now focus on your jaw, sensing it becoming loose and relaxed. . . . Now your face is relaxing, feeling warm and heavy . . . all the muscles around your eyes, relaxing . . . all around your head, loosening and relaxing. . . . Feel the muscles releasing their knots, the anxiety and tension flowing down and out.

Now, take a few moments to scan through your body, noting any remaining tension. . . . Release it now, and let it flow down and out. . . . Allow yourself to enjoy this relaxation and peacefulness.

Relax even deeper. . . . Allow your mind to become calm and peaceful. . . . Remember, you can send thoughts and feelings drifting away. . . . Focus on your feelings of deep, peaceful relaxation.

Now go even deeper. . . . Imagine yourself in a very special and safe place where you can be alone and at peace. . . . You can create your safe place and change it any way you like at any time. . . . Maybe it's a secluded place in nature, such as an ocean beach with gentle waves lapping at the shore, or a forest clearing with the comfortable sounds of birds . . . or perhaps a mountain meadow with a soft breeze whispering through the wildflowers . . . any place where you feel comfortable and safe.

Look around your safe place. . . . Sense the shapes and colors coming into focus, becoming more and more clear. . . . Notice what time of day it is—perhaps the soft light of morning or the colorful setting sun. . . . Listen to the sounds of nature around you. . . . Notice the fragrance in the air. . . . Feel the earth under your feet, or run your fingers through the water that might be there.

Make any changes you like; this is your place. . . . No one can come here without your invitation. . . . You are in control. . . . It feels good. . . . Let any distracting thoughts float away.

Now come back to full awareness of the room around you . . . feeling refreshed. . . . Allow your eyes to slowly open. . . . Take a few slow, deep breaths, and enjoy the moment.

Now you're ready to learn how to master your distressing feelings so they no longer interfere with your success and your interactions with others. In the next chapter, I'll show you how to heal the pain of losing your job. I will review the emotional closure scenario of the Job-Loss Recovery Program and provide you with the four steps leading to emotional mastery.

CHAPTER 5

Mastering Distressing Emotions

Anger as soon as fed is dead—
'Tis starving that makes it fat.

—Emily Dickinson

Closure Is Critical

Logically, you may be able to understand why companies, in the throes of downsizing, restructuring, and merging, lay off employees. Many companies have run into financial hardship and must find ways to survive. Layoffs are generally not personal, having very little to do with performance evaluations. You may understand this and may even have stoically thought, "This is just part of life, and the only thing constant in life is change."

Of course that's true. Yet, at the same time, you may hear a nagging voice inside shouting, "But they shouldn't have the right to turn my life upside down like this! How do they get away with doing this to people?"

Job loss can ignite anger toward a past employer or shame and rage over vulnerability. These feelings can lead to a need to blame and punish or to create destructive fantasies directed toward anyone connected to the job's termination. If this has happened to you, these thoughts and feelings very likely conflict with your sense of conscience and lead to guilt or shame over such aggressive impulses.

These feelings are normal, however, and having them doesn't make you a bad person. We are complex human beings, subject to many kinds of emotions. Although you wouldn't really consider acting out your destructive fantasies, denying and suppressing them will impede your ability to move on. And as you know, suppressed feelings may also leak into your job-search interactions and sabotage your goals.

Imagine you're an interviewer listening to a candidate discuss prior experience with his or her company, and you clearly sense an underlying resentment toward the former employer. Do you want to add this person to your team? Probably not. In fact, many employers say they consider attitude even more important than resume.

I know this is true, based on my former experience as an executive search consultant. Companies hired me to recruit and interview job candidates for available management positions, and I learned to identify individuals who harbored unresolved issues about their former employers. Experience taught me these people weren't first-choice candidates.

For example, when I interviewed Janet, jobless for a month since her layoff, she presented an impressive resume and great references. Janet had most recently worked for five years as a department director with a high-tech company in Orange County. She appeared capable and enthusiastic, and I arranged to have her meet one of my client companies.

Executives from the company interviewed Janet on three separate occasions but finally decided it wouldn't work out. Some probing on my part revealed that she had a chip on her shoulder that was not immediately apparent and, as a result, wouldn't fit well into the company.

When I discussed attitude with Janet, she expressed surprise but seemed to understand. She then told me the story of her layoff. As she was arriving at her office one morning, Janet's supervisor met her at the door. He was flanked by two security guards, and he told her about the beginning of a wave of layoffs that had eliminated her position. Janet was stunned and became even more so when her supervisor requested she gather her personal belongings and leave immediately. The guards escorted Janet out of the building. She hadn't seen it coming and felt disrespected, belittled, and very angry.

> REACH CLOSURE TO AVOID TAKING UNWANTED
> EMOTIONS INTO YOUR JOB SEARCH.

In the ensuing weeks, Janet's upsetting feelings continued, and she had no idea how to resolve them. Instead, she did her best to ignore them and move on. It's no wonder Janet's underlying resentment seeped into her interviews.

Another result of emotional suppression is that no one can squelch one emotion without affecting all others. Not allowing yourself to experience grief effectively blocks your ability to feel positive emotions, as well. It then becomes extremely difficult to muster the energy and enthusiasm needed to execute the most effective job search.

Have you ever felt truly depressed? I mean for days or weeks at a time, not just for an hour or two. If so, it may have felt as if you lived in a void, cut off from all emotions except sadness and hopelessness, and removed from the world. You probably couldn't feel anything very deeply—neither anger nor enthusiasm. You likely felt stuck and couldn't seem to get motivated to accomplish anything. Depression is often the result of unexpressed anger.

My point is that you don't do yourself any favors by suppressing painful feelings. Humans are distinguished from the animal kingdom largely by our emotions. We are fundamentally emotional beings, as much as we sometimes like to deny it and as painful as it can be.

How then can you avoid taking oppressive emotions into the job search and job interviews, where they can prevent successful performance? By first reaching the emotional-acceptance stage of the grieving process, bringing closure to any painful feelings. What you intensely feel, you can then release.

Four Steps to Emotional Mastery

The Emotional Closure script of the MIT program will guide you through four steps designed to help heal your grief. By learning to master your emotions, you can make them work for rather than against you.

You can honor your emotional self in a way that will set you free by using this four-step process to emotional closure and healing. You can achieve resolution as you move through the steps of this script, which are to

1. *Recognize* your true feelings.

2. *Acknowledge* and express your true feelings safely.

3. *Forgive* others and/or yourself.

4. *Change* which emerges from the previous three steps. Make new choices for growth and positive possibilities.

Recognition

First, consciously recognize what you truly feel. That seemingly simple step may be difficult if you habitually have turned away from emotion, refusing to acknowledge any uncomfortable feelings. Getting in touch with those feelings may also be a little scary, and that's understandable. After all, no one wants to feel destabilizing stress and pain. The controlled, conscious way you will be dealing with your feelings in this program, however, ensures that you won't get carried away with emotion. Understand that you may have accumulated many different feelings related to your job loss, now indistinguishable from each other and milling about just below the surface of your consciousness. General anxiety often results. Recognizing your feelings is the first step toward relief.

Take a moment now to identify your various feelings. If you need prompting, look back at the list of job-loss grief symptoms in chapter 1, and at your responses to the Level of Distress Questionnaire. Make a note in your Journal of the different feelings you can identify within yourself.

If you're having difficulty recognizing your specific feelings, go to appendix B and do Exercise 1: Recognizing Your Feelings. Do that now.

Acknowledgment

The second step to bringing closure to these feelings is to acknowledge or own them. *Accept them as your feelings.* This step usually involves expressing them in some safe way, with a preplanned time for your expressing, which will take place shortly in the Module 1 program script. You will imagine expressing your feelings to someone responsible for the loss of your job and will receive a satisfactory response.

Emily Dickinson made an important point with just a few words, which I quoted at the start of this chapter: "Anger as soon as fed is dead. 'Tis starving that makes it fat." In other words, anger dissipates when expressed appropriately. On the other hand, anger is exacerbated when it's unacknowledged or suppressed.

As you think of the moment you were laid off, the feelings that erupted within you at that time may bubble up. Images retain the emotions originally associated with them. In this program, you will reenact the imagery of that moment in what feels like a satisfying way to you, and more empowering feelings will replace the distressing ones. Receiving the response that you wanted can heal a stronghold of painful emotions. Thus, control of the imagery gives you control of your emotions.

For example, assume you think the boss specifically selected you for layoff instead of a certain colleague, despite the colleague's poor job performance compared to yours. In the emotional-resolution scenario of this program, you might imagine telling off the boss and then listening while they apologize, explaining how your absence left a great void because of the high value the department placed on you. Or maybe you can imagine that a superior reamed them for letting you go.

When you immerse yourself in the scenario using all five senses, the subconscious will believe it's occurring in your outer reality and will support all of the steps toward emotional healing. You'll soon see the results.

In your Journal, make a list of all the people related to your job loss to whom you would like to speak your mind. It may include a former supervisor, the company president, colleagues left behind, or any number of others.

Forgiveness

That brings us to the third step, forgiveness. Most of us know that to forgive those who have injured us in any way is the right thing to do. The old adage "Forgive and forget" makes a lot of sense, because unless we do forgive, we cannot truly forget. You may not realize that the forgiver always benefits more than the one being forgiven.

Stanford University professors have done some interesting research on forgiveness. Fred Luskin, who heads up the Stanford Forgiveness Project research, believes forgiveness has great emotional and physical benefit. His studies show that learning to forgive produces healthier people.

Luskin provides three steps for learning the process of forgiveness (Dolbee 2001). The first step is to not rush it. Pushing to forgive before allowing yourself to really experience the hurt feelings thwarts your ability to forgive honestly and sincerely.

Therefore, when I suggest in the Emotional Closure script that you forgive those who have caused you pain, don't do it until you can do it honestly and sincerely. If you forgive by rote, without thought for meaning, you may as well not forgive at all.

WHEN YOU FORGIVE SOMEONE, YOU BENEFIT MORE THAN THE ONE FORGIVEN.

Luskin's second step is to realize that forgiveness is about you, not the offender. In other words, forgive to heal your own life. When you hold a grudge or harbor other negative feelings, you stay emotionally connected to the offender. Forgiving sets you free.

The third step is learning to not dwell on the pain inflicted by others. Look for the beauty and the positives in others and in life. Please do not interpret this to mean you should turn away from—avoid or deny—any emotional pain you honestly feel. Learning how to process painful feelings in order to release them is the objective.

When actively seeking the positive, you'll notice how circumstances that once caused great wounds don't arise nearly as often. And when those situations do arise, you will frequently choose a different response. For example, the next time you have a negative run-in with someone, you may not feel hurt at all, or you may have discovered how to process the hurt and do away with it quickly.

Don't confuse forgiveness with justice. Forgiveness doesn't mean condoning bad or illegal actions. Even after forgiving someone, you can still seek justice, when warranted.

Remember, you may need to forgive *yourself* as well as others. Anger directed inward sabotages self. It damages both confidence and self-esteem and can therefore negatively affect your job-search performance.

Mike came to me with four months of unemployment behind him. He had a background in sales and service in the high-tech industry, which included twelve years with a major telecommunications company. He'd earned an MBA in executive management and then accepted a better opportunity with another company. But eventually he was caught in a downsizing and laid off. Mike then secured a management position with another telecommunications company. Two years after he joined them, they merged with a corporation that retained their management staff following the merger. Once again, Mike was laid off. When he saw the *Fortune Magazine* article about my career-transition program, he clipped it out, but then forgot about it. Months of unemployment later, it turned up under a stack of papers, and Mike called me.

MAKE NEW CHOICES FOR A NEW FUTURE.

When I spoke with him, Mike was looking for a more stable industry where his skills would be transferable. He alluded to "all the degradation" he had experienced in his job search and told me he felt "battered down." I noticed that Mike didn't speak harshly or resentfully about any of his former employers. On the contrary, he said they did what they had to do. "I don't begrudge them for any of it. And I probably should have seen it coming." He blamed himself for not being prepared and for not beginning a job search before being forced to do so. He also blamed himself for putting his entire 401k portfolio in company stock rather than diversifying it.

Mike reproached himself, just as you may be placing blame on your own actions or reactions to your circumstances. You must process that blame just as surely as if it were directed at someone else.

To accomplish this, imagine yourself as the target in the Module 1 exercise, and express your feelings to yourself as you would to someone else. Follow through, as well, with receiving a satisfactory response and forgiving yourself when you're ready to do so. After all, you probably did what you thought was best at the time. Forgiving yourself is critical to freely and successfully moving on.

Now look at the list of your feelings and the people you want to talk to that you made in the previous section. To this list, add all those you want to forgive, even though you may not feel like you can forgive them at the moment. Include yourself, if applicable.

Change

The fourth step in the process of emotional closure is to change. Once you've recognized your true feelings, acknowledged and safely expressed them, and forgiven yourself or others, you will be ready to make new choices for growth and positive possibilities in your career.

This step often emerges naturally when you've accomplished the previous three. Your choices will come from a place of new perspective—that of a confident self, free of constraining emotions and limited insight. Therefore, you can understand why the choices and decisions made at this point may vary greatly from those made while in the throes of pain.

In the next chapter, you'll learn about a straightforward technique called Meeting Your Future Self that can increase your satisfaction with life. You will then begin Module 1.

CHAPTER 6

Meeting Your Successful Future Self

Dream big dreams! Imagine that you have no limitations, and then decide what's right, before you decide what's possible.

—Brian Tracy

Moving toward Your Future Self

Research has shown that envisioning successful Future Selves—or possible selves—increases effort and persistence and improves performance. This simple process has also been linked to an increase in life satisfaction. Internally meeting your possible Future Self can bring mental, emotional, and behavioral benefits.

In other words, you can direct your own growth and development through the mental construction of one or more possible Future Selves. The process begins with your self-image and takes on components that represent what you could become and what you'd like to become in the future.

Let's say you worked in middle management in your last position. You were doing well, had high self-esteem, and set a realistic career goal of becoming vice president. You had a strong desire for the position and could so clearly imagine being in that role with your company that you already felt a sense of satisfaction and accomplishment.

You were, in fact, envisioning your Future Self as vice president, although you may not have been consciously aware of the process. My point is that you can now direct and use this practice to your significant advantage.

When you hold an image of having reached a desired goal, that vision produces a processing of information leaning toward the goal. You begin to feel more in control of your situation, and it then becomes possible to formulate more efficient plans to create it. As a result, the probability of actually creating it increases, especially if you can anticipate and experience the feelings associated with—and have strong desire for—the final result. It's easy to understand why envisioning a successful Future Self is often associated with improved performance.

In three studies, all relating imagery to performance, researchers Ruvolo and Markus (1992) found that people who imagined themselves as future successes outperformed those who imagined themselves as future failures.

In the first study, they specifically examined the effects of guided imagery tasks. They designed three conditions for comparison and randomly assigned the 105 undergraduates who participated.

··◆ Condition 1 imagined having success in the future because of hard work.

··◆ Condition 2 imagined being unsuccessful in the future despite hard work.

··◆ Condition 3 participants were put in a good mood (control group, no imagery).

On a subsequent task involving effort, as well as a task involving persistence, those who imagined being successful clearly performed the best.

The other two studies were variations of the first. In both, participants who imagined being successful in the future outperformed those who imagined being unsuccessful.

In summary, envisioning success promotes the development of plans and strategies necessary for achieving success. In the process, you become more motivated to make it happen and can often overcome any related anxiety, fear, and lack of self-confidence.

By the same token, imagining failure works the same way. For this reason, you certainly don't want to give energy to images of failure. So be sure to monitor your thoughts and take responsibility for your mental images.

We often have multiple ideas and images of who we can become and what we can accomplish in this lifetime. Career transition is an excellent time to explore those ideas to aid in determining where your greatest interests and talents lie and to develop clarity about the direction you want to take. Knowing what you want will allow you to focus your efforts more successfully on your job search. It will also make you a more desirable job candidate. Yogi Bera once said, "If you don't know where you're going, you'll end up someplace else."

Take a moment to do a short, supplemental exercise before meeting your happiest and most successful Future Self in the Module 1 program script. It is Exercise 2 in appendix B, called "Recognizing Future Possibilities." The exercise is designed for you to try out several different images of what your future might look like. In it, you'll imagine two or three possible Future Selves.

If you already feel intensely committed to a particular direction, you may want to skip this exercise. However, it could still provide you with valuable information about yourself.

Sarah's Progress

Do you remember Sarah, the young woman I introduced in chapter 2? She had been laid off for seven months when she came to me. She'd had no MIT experience and some skepticism about the program. She'd held a high-paying job in the high-tech industry and had resorted to waitressing to survive. Sarah was desperate and willing to try anything.

Before you embark on your journey of discovery and healing, I would like to share Sarah's progressive healing experience with Module 1 of the Job-Loss Recovery Program. She wrote about her thoughts and feelings after every session and has given me permission to share her journal.

Session 1

Very soon after I began to relax I was able to almost lose feeling in my body as I slipped into my safe place. It took me a while to decide what my safe place would be, but I was able to find one and be happy with my choice. I was able to bring myself back to the day of my dismissal, and

I was surprised as to how much I remembered about that day. I remembered all the feelings that I had, and I was able to admit things that I had pushed away. The resentment and disbelief came flooding back. I told my boss how disappointed I was about her inability to be honest with me, how she should have fought for me, or how she should have at least let me fight for my job. I let her know that I thought her behavior was wimpy. I let her apologize, since I know she did feel bad. I told her how bad I felt that she didn't keep in touch with me, and she said it was because she didn't feel right about the experience. I like picturing my future self. She looked a lot like my former self: successful, in control, effective, likeable. She had presence. And I realized that I was still that person. But she was different. She was calmer, knew herself better, and had other things in her life besides a career. She was more open, nurturing, at home in her own body. She was happy and content.

When I came out of the reverie I noticed how relaxed I was. I wanted to stay in my safe place a little longer and spend more time with my future self. I liked picturing the future. I felt more calm and forgiving of myself. I felt that it was important to start believing in myself again.

Session 2

This time I fell even deeper into the reverie. Unfortunately, my thoughts drifted a little more than the first time, so I had to gently concentrate on focusing on the visualization exercise. But I also was able to think of different things to say to my boss about her behavior and choices. I'm beginning to feel a lot less resentment and more confident in myself and my talents and skills. I'm realizing that the job loss wasn't my fault and that there was nothing I could do to prevent it. I know I really need to focus on my strengths and not focus on what happened in the past. It's time to move on and believe in myself again, like all the people in my life do. When I pictured my future self this time, I also let my thoughts go, but I'm not even sure where they went. I do know that I can achieve my dreams instead of focusing on how I'm going to pay my rent and how my career has changed. I need to really believe that I can achieve my goals and that I deserve success because I've earned it.

Session 3

This session further cemented my belief in myself. I even felt that my future self was me, now. I believed that I had all the skills and feelings of my future self, that all I needed now was the chance to prove myself. I used to be so self-confident—a feeling that I had because I was excellent at my job—and I need to regain those feelings. I am still the same person that I was, and I'm really starting to believe that. I feel stronger, more capable of pushing myself to realize my dreams.

You'll hear more from Sarah in chapter 8.

Implementing Module 1

You're now ready to implement Module 1, which is comprised of the first three MIT sessions in the Job-Loss Recovery Program. The module includes relaxation plus the following two scripts: Emotional Closure and Meeting Your Future Self. Below, an introduction to each of the scenarios provides a summary and suggestions to make your sessions even more powerful. The complete script for Module 1 follows the introduction.

Your imagery skills and, therefore, the impact of your sessions will improve with use. If you haven't used MIT before, I recommend you practice a few brief exercises before you implement Module 1. These supplemental exercises were designed to sharpen your imagery skills and can be found in appendix B. They're grouped in Exercise 3: Refining Your Imagery Skills. Do them now.

As your MIT experiences become more three-dimensional and encompass all five senses, they will become more *associated* than *dissociated*. What I mean is that, in the beginning, it will probably seem as if you're watching yourself move through the scenarios on your mind's internal screen. In other words, you'll be more dissociated from the action. In this state, the images are typically vague and unclear. Later, as you become intimately involved by using your senses and emotions in the scenarios, you'll feel more associated, as if they're actually happening to you now, rather than to someone you're watching.

At times, you will want to use both states. For example, in the emotional-closure scenario of your first session, you'll begin from a dissociated perspective and then shift into an associated perspective. First, you'll see yourself through a window in your safe place—a dissociated experience. Then you'll imagine moving through the window and into the scene, directly acting out the scene as it happens to *you*—an associated experience. As your sessions become more associated, they become powerful tools for transformation.

Evaluating the Impact

The statements listed below refer to your experiences of program sessions. Using the following scale, from 1 to 7, where 1 equals "I do not agree at all" and 7 equals "I agree extremely," place the corresponding number to the left of each of the following statements.

           1   2   3   4   5   6   7
I do not agree at all   I agree extremely

____ Overall, in my session(s), I felt my emotions deeply.

____ Overall, the images in my session(s) were vivid and specific.

____ My focus and involvement in the session(s) were very deep.

____ I have experienced deep relxation in my session(s).

____ My sessions(s) were highly meaningful to me.

____ **Total your score here.**

The total score amount is to be used for comparison only. You want to see an upward trend in subsequent scores over the course of the program. As your scores increase, expect the positive impact of the program experiences to increase as well.

Module 1 Script Introduction

The first half of the program—Module 1—includes two key experiences, summarized below. Remember that all of your sessions will begin with the Basic Relaxation Skills script.

Emotional Closure

To begin Module 1, you will breathe deeply and slowly, relax your muscles, and go to your safe place. There you will see a large, one-way window. You can see yourself through the window at your former job, perhaps when you first felt something was wrong or when you were told you would be laid off. It's your choice. Feel yourself being gently drawn through the window into the scene. There, you can express your thoughts and feelings safely, restoring justice and balance without fear of retaliation. You will also receive a response that is satisfactory to you and have the opportunity to forgive yourself or someone else—when you're ready.

When executing your sessions, adapt selected segments of the script to your specific situation. For example, when the script refers to speaking your mind to a former boss, you may want to make it the company president, a former colleague, or even yourself.

Meeting Your Future Self

You will then meet and interact with the most ideal, successful, wise, and loving self you can now imagine becoming in this lifetime. It may be one you met in the exercise, or it may be one you haven't yet imagined or thought possible. Using your imagination in this way stretches your limits of what you can conceive as possible. You will also receive a gift from your Future Self. It may be tangible or not—an object, a symbol, a word or thought. The gift can open possibilities to advance you on your path to becoming more of this Future Self.

Alternate Program Structure

The Job-Loss Recovery Program is organized in the exact structure that was used in my job-loss study. The structure's proven success warranted no change.

When I initially created the study protocol, I knew the program had to be compact, as well as quick and easy to implement. Otherwise, displaced employees would never agree to complete it, and I would have no study participants. So I combined the program scenarios to make two modules to achieve the program's goals with fewer sessions than by stringing out the scenarios in single sessions. For example, Emotional Closure and Meeting Your Future Self are experienced in one session as Module 1, rather than as individual sessions. I then instructed participants to repeat each of the two modules three times, the minimum amount of repetitions to yield success based on my experience and education.

However, since you're not a study participant, you may prefer to take a little more time to complete the program than they did. I've developed an alternate program structure you may follow if that is your preference. In that case, each of your sessions would include one fewer experience and, as a result, it would take twelve sessions rather than six to complete the program.

To help you make the better choice for you, I'll list some considerations for each. Let's call the original structure Choice A, and the alternate structure Choice B. You may want to review the structure of Choice A on page 38.

Choice A

··• The program can be completed quickly, in six days.

··• The structure proved successful in the study.

··• In Module 1, being with your wisest and happiest Future Self immediately after expressing your most uncomfortable feelings in the Emotional Closure scenario can be extremely uplifting.

··• In Module 2, interacting with your Mentor immediately after rehearsing job interviews may supply feedback and insights to improve your next interview rehearsal.

Choice B

··• Sessions are shorter, which is important if you find it difficult to put aside twenty minutes at a time.

··➡ If you choose not to record the scripts for playback, sessions with fewer scenarios may be simpler to remember and implement.

With Choice B, the first session begins with the Basic Relaxation Skills plus Emotional Closure scripts. The second session includes the Basic Relaxation Skills plus Future Self scripts. Sessions 3 and 4 and sessions 5 and 6 are repeats of sessions 1 and 2, in that order. Repetition is still important to success. Scripts for relaxation and each scenario appear individually in appendix A, for convenience.

Sessions for Choice B will be organized in the following way:

Sessions 1, 3, and 5

··➡ Basic Relaxation and Safe Place

··➡ Emotional Closure

Sessions 2, 4, and 6

··➡ Basic Relaxation and Safe Place

··➡ Meeting Your Future Self

Sessions 7, 9, and 11

··➡ Basic Relaxation and Safe Place

··➡ Mentally Rehearsing a Job Interview

Sessions 8, 10, and 12

··➡ Basic Relaxation and Safe Place

··➡ Meeting Your Mentor

To sum up, you may want to go with Choice A—beginning now with the following Module 1 script—if you prefer a proven program structure and if speed of completion is critical to you. Select Choice B—using scripts in the book's appendix—if you prefer to focus on only one experience per session and if you are willing to take six additional days to complete the program.

Module 1 Script: Relaxation, Emotional Closure, Meeting Your Future Self

Find a comfortable position. . . . Gently close your eyes. Begin by focusing on your breathing—inhaling deeply and exhaling fully. . . . Allow your abdomen to expand and contract as you breathe deep into your diaphragm. . . . And again . . . breathing in relaxation . . . and breathing out any tension in your body. . . . Inhale . . . exhale . . . relaxing more and more . . . becoming more calm with every breath. . . . Imagine any distracting thoughts drifting away. . . . For the moment, your mind is still . . . feeling calm and relaxed now . . . inhaling deeply . . . and exhaling.

Enjoy these few moments in peaceful relaxation. . . . Notice the heaviness as your muscles begin to relax. . . . As I count down from ten to one, allow yourself to become more and more relaxed. . . . Imagine all the anxiety flowing out of you as you relax deeper and deeper. . . . Ten, nine, eight, going deeper, seven, six, five, four, going even deeper, three, two, one. Very good. . . . Allow these feelings of relaxation to spread through your body. . . . You may notice a warm, heavy feeling coming over you, a sign of deep relaxation.

Now move your attention to your feet. . . . Feel all the muscles in your feet and toes slowly relax, and begin to feel very loose and warm. . . . Allow the relaxation to spread into your calves as these muscles begin to feel loose, warm, and heavy. . . . Now release any tension you feel in your knees. . . . Now feel your thigh muscles begin to relax, all the tension releasing down, out of your feet, and into the earth. . . . This relaxing, peaceful feeling is a gift you're giving to yourself.

Now focus on your hips and abdomen. . . . Feel all the muscles loosening and relaxing. . . . Release any tension held there, allowing it to flow down and out of your body. . . . Now your back muscles are loosening, feeling warm. . . . Your neck and shoulders, a favorite place to hold burdens, are loosening and releasing any knots blocking you. . . . Continue to relax as you go deeper and deeper.

Move your attention to your arms, your upper and lower arms, and your hands. . . . Let go of any burdens and responsibilities. You can pick them up again later. . . . Sense your hands relaxing and warming as the tension flows out through your fingers. . . . Now focus on your jaw, sensing it becoming loose and relaxed. . . . Now your face is relaxing, feeling warm and heavy . . .

all the muscles around your eyes, relaxing . . . all around your head, loosening and relaxing. . . . Feel the muscles releasing their knots, the anxiety and tension flowing down and out.

Now, take a few moments to scan through your body, noting any remaining tension. . . . Release it now, and let it flow down and out. . . . Allow yourself to enjoy this relaxation and peacefulness.

Relax even deeper. . . . Allow your mind to become calm and peaceful. . . . Remember, you can send thoughts and feelings drifting away. . . . Focus on your feelings of deep, peaceful relaxation.

Now go even deeper. . . . Imagine yourself in a very special and safe place where you can be alone and at peace. . . . You can create your safe place and change it any way you like at any time. . . . Maybe it's a secluded place in nature, such as an ocean beach with gentle waves lapping at the shore, or a forest clearing with the comforting sounds of birds . . . or perhaps a mountain meadow with a soft breeze whispering through the wildflowers . . . any place where you feel comfortable and safe.

Look around your safe place. . . . Sense the shapes and colors coming into focus, becoming more and more clear. . . . Notice what time of day it is—perhaps the soft light of morning or the colorful setting sun. . . . Listen to the sounds of nature around you. . . . Notice the fragrance in the air. . . . Feel the earth under your feet, or run your fingers through the water that might be there.

Make any changes you like; this is your place. . . . No one can come here without your invitation. . . . You are in control. . . . It feels good. . . . Let any distracting thoughts float away, as you go even deeper.

Now, out of the corner of your mental eye, something captures your attention, and you turn to see a large window somewhere in your safe place. . . . Curious, you move toward it and somehow know this is a one-way window into your world. . . . You can see through it to the other side, but no one can see you. . . . As you look through the window, a scene begins to come into focus. . . . You realize this is you at your former job . . . perhaps when you were told you would be laid-off. . . . You choose the scene.

Now feel yourself being gently drawn through the window and sense yourself there. . . . It may seem like a long time ago, or like yesterday. . . . Look around. . . . Listen to the sounds, perhaps of people talking or of computers or other equipment operating. . . . Mentally reach out and touch something in your environment. Perhaps you slide your fingers across a desk. . . . How did you feel at the time? . . . Others, when laid off, have often felt shock at

*first, then anger or sadness, anxiety, fear, guilt, or even
embarrassment. . . . How did you respond? What actions did you
take? . . . Or did you do nothing? . . . Are you angry or resentful?
. . . If you are, is it toward others? Or perhaps you're mad at
yourself for being vulnerable and losing control of your career.*

*Now invite into your scene, if they're not already there,
anyone to whom you want to express your thoughts and feelings
without fear of retaliation. . . . Who is there is your choice. . . .
Sense them with you, and greet them in your own way. . . . Notice
their expressions, their clothing. . . . Remember how you felt. . . .
Notice how you feel now. . . . Now set your intention on mentally
saying anything you want to say and doing anything you want to
do but with no actual intent to harm anyone in reality. . . . As a
symbol of your intention to harm no one, sense a protective shield
or bubble around you and the other person or persons in your
scene.*

*Mentally say what is on your mind. . . . Don't think about
choosing your words carefully. . . . Simply express your feelings. . . .
If you feel angry, abandoned, or betrayed, tell them about it as
they listen intently to you. . . . If you have mixed feelings, express
the ambivalence as well . . . perhaps the sadness of losing contact
with friends . . . along with anticipation of new opportunities. . . .
You may be surprised at some of the feelings that surface within
you. . . . Anything you feel is okay. . . . Simply say and do anything
you want. . . . Let it all go. . . . Reach deep within you and release
it all. . . . Take as long as you like to do that. It feels good to
release what you have been holding onto. . . . You may feel a sense
of relief.*

*Now, how would you prefer to have this person or these
people respond to you? . . . Remember, you are writing the
script. . . . Listen as they respond in exactly that way. . . . Take as
long as you like. . . . How does that feel? . . . Don't label it, simply
feel it, allowing the feeling to wash over and through you. . . .
Now, if you like, impose upon them whatever retribution you feel
is fair and just. . . . It's entirely your choice. . . . Now is your
chance. . . . Go for it. You are in control . . . and you're not
harming anyone in reality. . . . They do not resist or retaliate in any
way. . . . Take the time you need to do that. . . . They may even
apologize. . . . If they do, accept the apology or not, as you like . . .
perhaps even forgive . . . only when you're ready.*

*Think of your safe place now, and find yourself there once
again . . . perhaps with expanded perspective. . . . Maybe you
discovered anger you hadn't realized was there. . . . Perhaps you*

surprised yourself by forgiving and feel a weight lifting off you. . . .
You are learning more about who you are. . . . You know, too, that
you are doing your best, and that new opportunities for work and
growth are not limited. . . . If one passes, another will reveal
itself. . . . You know that challenges are a part of life's journey and
that you have the skills to successfully move through and beyond
them.

Now, out of the corner of your mental eye, you notice
someone standing in shadow at the edge of your safe place. . . .
Curious, you move closer. . . . This person looks amazingly like you,
yet somehow different. . . . You realize now that this is you at some
point in your future, perhaps ten years hence, or maybe even
twenty to thirty years from now. . . . This Future Self represents the
epitome of your potential self—the most wise, the most loving, the
most happy and successful self you can become in this lifetime.

Invite your Future Self into your safe place . . . and as the
figure slowly approaches . . . coming more into focus . . . look for
details. . . . You may or may not see the image clearly—it doesn't
matter. . . . Simply sense the essence and existence of this future
you. . . . Sense the connection between you. . . . Greet one another
in whatever way feels right for you, perhaps a touch or an
embrace.

And now look into the eyes of this Future Self, and feel the
warmth and loving support coming from one who truly knows
you. . . . See your current life through the perspective of those wise,
loving eyes. . . . Perhaps you're given a sense of what you are truly
capable of doing with your abilities in this lifetime. . . . Take a
little time to do that. Allow any feelings and images to wash over
you. . . . You might talk with your Future Self now, and listen
intently to the response. . . . Perhaps you ask for insight into your
progress with healing the emotional pain . . . or simply experience
being in one another's presence. . . . Take as much time as you
need.

Know that you will overcome your current challenges and will
be stronger and wiser for it. . . . Forgive yourself, as well as others,
for past failures or disappointments. . . . Now imagine having
received an offer for the position of your choice. . . . Feel the
pleasure of having successfully completed your search . . . and
imagine yourself celebrating with your loved ones. . . . Take the time
to enjoy that now.

Mentally feel the gentle squeeze of a hand on your arm as
your Future Self reaches out to you with a gift. . . . It may be an
object, a symbol, a word, or a thought . . . tangible or not. . . .

Allow it be what it is. . . . If it feels right to do so, simply accept it. . . . If you don't understand it, that's all right. . . . For now, it's enough to know that it comes with love.

In a moment, you will come back to full awareness of the room where your journey began, feeling relaxed and refreshed. . . . The count of three, two, one will help you return. . . . Three . . . begin to return, sense the feelings in your body . . . two, sense the environment around you, and begin to move around . . . and one. When you are ready, open your eyes and return, feeling awake and refreshed. . . . Take a few slow, deep breaths, stretch if you like, and enjoy the moment.

After Completing Module 1

After you've completed three sessions of Module 1 (or six sessions if you selected the twelve-session structure of Choice B), please again complete the Level of Distress Questionnaire. Compare your scores with those you obtained before beginning the program. You should feel closure on the job-related issues that formerly disturbed you, and your stress level should have significantly decreased. Understand that closure isn't "all or nothing" at this point. You may feel resolved over-all, yet distress may pop through, from time to time, for a while. Expect continued improvement through Module 2.

If you'd like the satisfaction of tracking the development of your imagery skills throughout the program, the Level of Distress Question-naire should be followed by the Evaluating the Impact scale. Rate yourself after the first program session, again at the midpoint, and once again after the last session. Keep track of your scores. Feel free to complete it after every program session if you like. You may want to make copies of the scale for that purpose.

I have found that the five statement ratings typically move up together. As you relax more deeply, for instance, your focus will also deepen, permitting you to become more involved in the sessions's sce-narios. The experiences, in turn, well become more meaningful to you.

If you have an off day, when the impact scores are a little lower than before, don't worry about it. Remember, you're looking for an improving trend over the course of the program.

Level of Distress Questionnaire

The statements listed below refer to your inner feelings in regard to your job loss. Using the following scale from 1 to 10, insert the number that most closely reflects your current feelings and state of mind.

1	2	3	4	5	6	7	8	9	10
Never		*Sometimes*			*Frequently*			*Most of the Time*	

_____ I have trouble focusing on what I am doing.

_____ I feel anxious.

_____ I feel frustrated.

_____ I have waves of distressing feelings.

_____ I am reminded of my job loss often.

_____ I try to ignore my feelings about my job loss.

_____ I feel depressed.

_____ I have trouble staying motivated.

_____ I feel angry and/or resentful.

_____ I have trouble sleeping because I keep thinking about my job loss.

_____ I feel fearful.

_____ Any reminder brings back stressful feelings.

_____ I have troubling dreams about my job loss.

For this final statement, use a 1 to 10 scale but, this time, 1 indicates *Strongly Disagree* and 10 means *Strongly Agree*. Insert the number that most closely reflects your current belief, as is relevant to your job loss.

_____ Little can be done to change my job-related problems.

_____ **Total your score here.**

This score represents your current level of distress about your job loss and is for comparison purposes only.

Evaluating the Impact

The statements listed below refer to your program-session experiences. Using the following scale, from 1 to 7, with "I agree not at all" being 1 to "I agree extremely" being 7, place the corresponding number to the left of each of the following statements.

	1	2	3	4	5	6	7	
I do not agree at all   I agree extremely

____ Overall, in my session(s), I felt my emotions deeply.

____ Overall, the images in my session(s) were vivid and specific.

____ My focus and involvement in the session(s) were very deep.

____ My experience of relaxation in my session(s) has been deep.

____ My sessions(s) were highly meaningful to me.

____ **Total your score here.**

The total score amount is to be used for comparison only. You want to see an upward trend in subsequent scores over the course of the program. As your scores increase, expect the positive impact of the program experiences to increase as well.

You may continue to benefit by repeating Module 1 beyond the three times suggested in the program, as Mike did in the last chapter. Because he had several unresolved issues dating back many years with his last company, he worked with Module 1 for six sessions before feeling full closure on his past.

If you continue to feel frequent distress or depression and don't yet feel resolved—even after further work with Module 1—consider therapeutic counseling as an additional resource.

Did you reach the point in the last MIT session where you could honestly forgive everyone involved in your job loss? If not, ask yourself the following questions:

···· Was it difficult to get emotionally involved in the MIT scenarios?

···· Was my entire perspective dissociated rather than associated?

If the answer is yes to either of these questions, practice the suggested Exercise 3: Refining Your Imagery Skills in appendix B, and execute Module 1 again. If you haven't yet become emotionally engaged in the program, ask yourself why you might be resisting. Answer as honestly as you can.

You've now completed Module 1 of the Job-Loss Recovery Program and are ready for Module 2. In chapter 7 you will learn how mental rehearsal has helped many others and how it can help you.

PART III

Getting the Job You Really Want: Module 2

CHAPTER 7

Rehearsing Your Success

Before everything else, getting ready is the secret of success.

—Henry Ford

Improving Self-Confidence and Competence

As you learned in chapter 2, mental rehearsal has burgeoned in popularity and is used in a number of areas of life. Why? Because it works! Many singers and actors use it to overcome stage fright, and both amateur and professional sports enthusiasts rely on mental imagery exercises to prepare for their sports events. I noted Jack Nicklaus's approach in chapter 2, and now, to inspire you to use mental rehearsal in preparing for your job interviews and other job-search activities, I'll offer even more evidence.

Kenneth Baum, a leading sports performance consultant and author of *The Mental Edge* (1999), relates that he occasionally encounters skepticism from athletes regarding the power of visualization. "But once they're aware of the impressive body of research into the mind-body connection, their hesitancy comes to a screeching halt that burns the rubber on the soles of their workout shoes" (25).

Coach and former gymnastics champion Terry Orlick, Ph.D., in his book, *In Pursuit of Excellence* (1990), tells how a member of the national archery team used visualization to prepare for international competition.

> A former world champion spoke of how, through imagery, she was able to transport herself to the world championship from her practice site. Instead of seeing the single target that was actually in front of her, she saw targets stretched across the field. She was fully aware of her competitors. On her right was the leading Polish archer; on her left, a German. She could see them, hear them, and feel them. She shot her rounds under these conditions in the same sequence as she would shoot in the real competition. She prepared herself for the competition and distractions by creating the world championships in imagery and by actually shooting under mentally simulated world championship conditions (75).

Twenty-three-year-old Kelly Wiglesworth, television's former *Survivor* contestant and river guide, has been quoted as saying "I do a lot of envisioning: If I want something bad enough, I picture myself making it happen—no matter how far-fetched it seems. I won five consecutive competitions on the island that way."

Mental rehearsal not only improves one's confidence and self-image, it also increases the perception of having control over a stressful situation. When we feel confident and in control, we're able to approach problems with greater clarity and insight, making it possible to manage our actions and any uncomfortable emotions more successfully.

In this scenario of the Job-Loss Recovery Program, you will mentally rehearse job interviews. I have chosen competitive sports as a basis for comparison because both successful sports achievement and successful interview achievement require the same key elements. For example, they are both competitive activities that demand constant focus and concentration. One must have a clear strategy yet be able to think and adapt quickly to changing circumstances.

Visualizing a successful interview performance will prepare you for the competitive environment and potential distractions of the interview situation. You will, of course, include interviewers in your visualization to make it as real as possible. As a result, when you do face a real interviewer, you'll appear as a polished, self-confident professional with a winning attitude.

WHEN YOU ARE CONFIDENT AND IN CONTROL, YOU CAN DEAL EFFECTIVELY WITH UNEXPECTED CIRCUMSTANCES.

Another well-documented use of imagery is mentally rehearsing a painful or anxiety-filled medical event to minimize its harmful impact on the mind and body. Courage, stamina, and the ability to face the unknown are required when faced with such an ordeal. Mental preparation results in keeping attention and energy focused and has effectively reduced pain and anxiety.

The treatment of severe burn injury, as an example, although very successful in saving lives, is frequently regarded as more stressful and painful than the injury itself. Wound care involves debridement—daily removal of the dead tissue from the wound with forceps and scissors. The process is among the most feared and painful of hospital procedures. Patients often describe the method as feeling like being skinned alive. Painkillers are avoided before the procedure, because patients must walk themselves to and from the locations in the hospitals where this process takes place. Exercise is critical to the healing.

In a large study using 149 severely burn-injured, hospitalized adults, Achterberg, Kenner, and Lawlis (1988) tested three methods of anxiety and pain control and compared them with a no-treatment control group. The methods were relaxation; combined relaxation and imagery; and combined relaxation, imagery, and biofeedback. (The main purpose of biofeedback is to control body functions, such as heart rate or blood pressure.) Each participant received six sessions of the appropriate method in conjunction with daily wound care.

The imagery plus relaxation combination resulted in less muscle tension and fewer pain medications and sedatives than the other groups. The researchers concluded that during acutely painful states, it's more important to learn mental techniques for dealing with the stressful situations than it is to control body functions.

Now, if mental rehearsal can help reduce pain and anxiety under these frightful conditions, surely it can help you remain calm and focused on a job interview.

I use mental rehearsal to prepare for a variety of circumstances. For instance, I recently spoke at the kickoff meeting of a businesswomen's organization. Once I had my presentation prepared, I practiced it using both oral and mental rehearsal. I imagined all the details, from being introduced and walking to the front of the room with a smile, to delivering an inspiring message and bonding with a receptive audience, to humbly accepting applause at the end—with the audience standing for me (of course).

But I was in for a surprise. When I arrived at the country-club location, the dinner meeting had been moved outside to the lawn, adjacent to the tennis courts. Registrations had far exceeded expectations, and there just wasn't room for everyone inside. By the time dinner ended and I was introduced, dusk was fast approaching and the tennis courts were lit. The audience faced the courts, located directly behind me. I couldn't imagine an arrangement more distracting for them, as well as for me.

Because I was well-prepared, I delivered my presentation as planned —and also took advantage of several opportunities to add humorous comments: when an insect flew into my eye and when the players shouted scores from the tennis courts. Even though the audience undoubtedly found it very difficult to make a strong connection with me under those conditions, I kept going. Had I not kept my composure and a positive attitude, the presentation could have ended in disaster. Needless to say, I didn't get the standing ovation I'd visualized, but I did a good job in an impossible situation.

Although I was unable to control external circumstances, I *could* control myself. Even after doing my best to mentally rehearse the event, it didn't happen exactly as I'd imagined it. But since I had done the groundwork, I felt confident in my ability to deal effectively with unexpected circumstances. In other words, I had a strong sense of self-efficacy.

Self-efficacy is the judgment that you have the capability to carry out the necessary actions to achieve selected goals or performances. It's not about skills but, rather, about the judgment of what you can do with the skills you have.

Low self-efficacy is often accompanied by fear, because the perceived inability to cope with harmful events makes them frightening. When you believe you can effectively deal with a potentially harmful event, such as job loss, you have no reason to fear it. As a result, life experiences or mental exercises that increase your belief in your abilities—your self-efficacy—shrink your fear as well.

For instance, when you successfully perform challenging skills in your mind while feeling positive emotions, your self-efficacy often improves—along with the determination to experience these emotions again in real situations. Anxiety and fear are often reduced as well (Smith 1990).

In *Who Moved My Cheese?* (1998), Spencer Johnson, M.D., tells a story about change that takes place in a maze where four little characters search for "cheese," which acts as a metaphor for anything we want in life, such as a job, money, a relationship, or whatever. One of the characters learned some important lessons as he searched for cheese, one of which was: "Imagining myself enjoying new cheese even before I find it, leads me to it" (58).

In the mental-rehearsal scenario of this program, you will picture yourself, in great detail, achieving and enjoying the position of your choice. The more clearly you can imagine yourself doing that, the more real and believable it will become.

The participants in my MIT job-loss study especially liked the interview-rehearsal component. Here are some poststudy comments.

"Currently feeling well prepared for future interviews. Expecting marked improvement on previous weak points."

"I enjoyed them [the sessions]. Feel confident in my ability to have successful interviews."

"Session 6: Was anticipating it being my last session and wanted to fully focus and experience the emotion, calm, and imagery of 'encounters.' Session was very pleasant and heartening."

"Great relaxation. Helps me relax during interviews. Able to visualize myself, and that helps project a better image during interviews."

"I felt confidence and, at times, even though I would have to rewind to correct or think about a convincing statement, I felt the interview was going perfectly."

"I like the idea. I will use it on my own—to play, pause, edit, my own interview movie without the time constraints."

"I liked this process. I felt a lot of positive energy in visualizing a successful interview."

"Very relaxing. In sessions 4 and 5, it was difficult to stay with the imaging of an interview, but by session 6, I was very focused, due to it being just before an anticipated interview for a consulting job."

In chapter 8, I show you how to gain new insights into your career and life to increase your confidence even more. You'll be provided with the Module 2 script of the Job-Loss Recovery Program, which includes mentally rehearsing job interviews. You will then implement Module 2.

CHAPTER 8

Meeting Your Mentor

If you are distressed by anything external, the pain is not due to the thing itself, but to your estimate of it; and this you have the power to revoke at any moment.

—Marcus Aurelius

Access Your Inner Wisdom

You are now ready to meet your inner Mentor, the final scenario in the Job-Loss Recovery Program. A mentor is part collaborator, part personal consultant, part cheerleader, and part sounding board. A mentor can help you take more responsibility for your own growth and development and can help you come to grips with huge changes— such as career transition. A mentor can also help you increase your self-confidence and motivation.

This inner Mentor can meet your special needs. For example, some people need a great deal of positive feedback, others need challenge; some need someone to hold them accountable, and still others simply need a sounding board.

Who or what is this inner Mentor, really? The concept comes from both eastern and western traditions, dating back thousands of years. It's been referred to by many names, such as the subconscious, inner wisdom, inner guide, guardian angel, and spirit guide. I like to call it the "Inner Mentor." Whatever you choose to call this guidance, you can access it if you honestly seek the truth within yourself. I have been amazed at the insight and understanding that comes from this source—in my clients and in myself.

Develop New Insight through Reframing

Your inner Mentor can help reframe and reappraise events and circumstances in your life. Reframing refers to redefining or reevaluating a situation from a different perspective—usually a more positive one that wasn't noticed before. In chapter 3 I told you my "broken-foot" story. Well, if I had viewed the situation as a tragedy, I might have wallowed in self-pity and thought the worst: "I won't be able to do the job, and my boss will fire me." That's considered a *negative frame*. Rather than wallow, I decided to make the best of the situation and get on with my obligation. As it turned out, the cast was a conversation starter that gave me an opening to build rapport with my new clients.

Reframing often leads to helpful new insights as well as to a more positive attitude. This is important, since job loss can negatively impact your view of yourself, as well as your view of the world. As you've advanced through this MIT program, you've had the opportunity to utilize the language and processes in the scripts to help you reframe the loss more positively and gain new insights about yourself and your circumstances. And as you develop optimistic perspectives, your confidence and motivation will increase.

Richard, the accountant from chapter 1, erroneously felt he deserved to lose his job, thinking it was his fault. His thoughts raced from "What if no employer wants me?" to "I could lose everything." He made a negative appraisal of his situation and, therefore, became anxious and depressed.

Reappraisal, as I mentioned in chapter 1, is the reevaluation of why and to what degree a situation is stressful. It's important to reexamine your initial appraisal of the job loss because you may find that a negative appraisal is the root cause of much of your stress. Understanding the underlying causes for feeling stress is the first step to disarming those causes.

When he reappraised his situation, Richard realized his greatest stress stemmed from his fear of financial ruin. He also learned to reframe his situation as a challenge and began to see that he already had valuable resources to support him through his transition, such as strong business skills and experience. Also among these resources that had been there all along was that his wife earned an income that could support them.

Richard also began to seriously consider starting a financial-consulting practice, something he'd always wanted to do. His family supported his dream, once they recovered from the initial shock of his job loss. As a result, Richard felt free to choose new goals and strategies that reflected more of who he really was and wanted to become. In other words, as Richard reframed his situation more positively and reappraised his resources, his depression lifted.

> ## REFRAMING JOB LOSS AS A CHALLENGE CAN AWAKEN NEW OPPORTUNITIES.

Reframing can also occur when you receive new information. Let's say you just returned from a preliminary interview for a position that appeals to you. The responsibilities fit well with your experience, the compensation package is good, and there appear to be sufficient challenges and opportunities for advancement. However, you don't really like the manager you'd be reporting to and, as a result, seriously consider not pursuing the position. Then you run into each other at the tennis club and you realize you have a shared interest. Maybe the manager's not so bad after all. The job opportunity starts looking more desirable. Based on this new information, you have reframed it.

Now that you're aware of the benefits of reframing and reappraising circumstances, you'll want to examine all the frames and appraisals you initially made around your job loss. This is one arena where your Mentor can help.

Your imagination can act as an effective substitute for real life. Your Mentor can provide a tremendous resource and force for your positive growth, if you are open to this concept.

Before you actually meet your Mentor, however, you will first rehearse a job interview. Your Mentor can then provide feedback on the interview as well as suggestions for improvement. But before we go on, let's revisit Sarah's journal to give you a sense of how one person experienced Module 2.

Sarah's Progress

Here are Sarah's impressions of Sessions 4, 5, and 6.

Session 4

Due to the helpful nature of Module 1, I was overjoyed to visualize an interview that had me performing without my previous defensiveness and lack of self-confidence. I was able to speak with a positive attitude and without offering any veiled apologies or excuses for my layoff and former inability to find another position. Even though my layoff wasn't my fault, I think I still behaved as if I had to explain it somehow, which came off as defensive and resentful. I just don't feel that way anymore. I think a company would be lucky to have me working for them and representing them. I was able to focus on my achievements and communicate them articulately and with confidence.

The mentor aspect was helpful for confidence reinforcement. I think I'll visualize this person even outside of the sessions whenever I need encouragement and a reminder of my talent and skills.

Session 5

Session 5 was good in that I was able to reinforce my intentions of focusing on the positive aspects of my career during a job interview. I could move away from feelings of resentment and a draining of self-esteem from the layoff. I visualized a friendly, positive, and effective job interview. And the reinforcement of my mentor, who praised me and reminded me of my past accomplishments, was helpful. I'm feeling more lighthearted, more positive, and more open to new possibilities. And I have a job interview tomorrow!

Session 6

This last session was extremely fruitful. I did it after a yoga class, which I think helped me relax even further. I really began to internally voice the idea of reinventing myself. It's becoming an action plan rather than simply a

*concept. I realize I need to work on the self-destructive
and negative voices in my head. I need to focus on
finding the sources of that voice in order to understand it
and overcome it. But I've made progress in that I also
realize how it has been affecting my life journey. Even
though I still worry about my future and other things (my
financial health, etc.), I'm feeling freer and more positive
about what I can accomplish. I'm able to turn my bad
moods around more quickly and to shake off the useless
feelings of despair that can grip me at any moment. I
have bad days, but I know they won't last if I gain
control over my feelings and emotions about myself. I
need to start feeling like superwoman again, and I think
I'm closer than I have been in a long time.*

As you can see, Sarah made great strides during her sessions.
Even though she had been out of work for seven months and was emotionally beaten down and depressed when she began, within thirty days
after her final session, she was back to work at a job she loved, thinking positively and feeling remarkably stronger. Sarah's experience promoted a journey to emotional health. If she can do it, you can too.

Implementing Module 2

You're now ready to implement Module 2, the final three sessions in
the Job-Loss Recovery Program. The module includes Basic Relaxation
Skills plus the following scenarios: Mentally Rehearsing a Job Interview and Meeting Your Mentor. The following introduction to each of
the scenario experiences will give you information and suggestions to
make the sessions have more impact. The complete script for Module
2 follows the introduction.

As with Module 1, I suggest recording the script for playback to
deepen and enhance the experience. Of course, you may choose to
implement the module by silently reading the script rather than
recording it and playing it back. However, it will be challenging to
reach and maintain the deep focus and concentration needed to receive
great benefit from the program if you attempt to immerse yourself in
the experience while reading the script.

Keep in mind that you should space the sessions at least one day
apart, as you did with Module 1.

A reminder: If you have chosen to implement each program scenario separately, rather than as a complete module, you'll find the scripts for each scenario included individually in appendix A. Begin with the mental-rehearsal scenario and then alternate it with the Mentor scenario until you've experienced each three times. And don't forget to begin each session with the Basic Relaxation Skills script.

Module 2 Script Introduction

The second half of the program—Module 2—includes two main experiences, summarized in this section. As before, each session begins with the Basic Relaxation Skills script.

Mentally Rehearsing a Job Interview

To begin Module 2, you will relax and go to your safe place. Again, the one-way window will be there, and you'll see yourself through the window, this time in an interview setting. If you have a real-life interview coming up, imagine that one. Otherwise, it can be any realistic interview that will take place in the future. You can then mentally direct the interview until it's satisfactory. An imaginary remote control device can be used as if the scene were a videotape. It can be stopped, rewound, or replayed, as you prefer.

This mental-rehearsal segment of the MIT session will take only about five minutes, after which you will replay the perfect interview—without stopping—from beginning to end, feeling a sense of control and satisfaction. Your logical mind may tell you that five minutes isn't long enough to make an impact. But remember that my study participants had only five minutes, and many noted this segment as one of the most valuable in the program. Take as long as you like with this exercise, however. The goal is to feel confident and prepared.

Use both dissociated and associated perspectives in your mental rehearsals. Dissociation occurs when you are in your safe place, watching and directing the interview through the window. With association, you experience the interview by acting out a scene, actually playing the role as you did in the emotional-resolution segment of the program.

As you begin an interview—observing, critiquing, editing, and replaying—you'll find the process easier to do from a dissociated state. If you find yourself being drawn into the scene at any time however, go with it. You can always move back to the dissociated state—step out of character, if you like—to edit the scene. When you're ready to play the entire scene without stopping, move into your character (the associated state) and give an enthusiastic performance that results in a job offer.

Although I've discussed mental rehearsal with a focus on interview preparation, it has extensive uses. Use your MIT sessions to rehearse and prepare for other job-search activities as well, such as making networking and referral calls.

Meeting Your Mentor

When you finish interviewing, your Mentor will be waiting at the edge of your safe place for your invitation to enter. You will not need to create this being as you did your Future Self. You will be in a relaxed state and comfortably sense or imagine your Mentor. He or she may represent an aspect of yourself, information from your unconscious, or an inner guide—if your beliefs support that idea. Perhaps this person is someone you admire in real life, alive now or not. You can choose who you want to mentor you, or you can trust your creative unconscious to present the person who can help you most, whoever that is.

One thing is certain. Your Mentor knows you, supports you, and may even love you. You'll imagine greeting him or her and settling comfortably somewhere in your safe place. The two of you can consult about current directions and challenges, or you may ask for an analysis of your interviews and other job-search activities, whether they occurred in fact or were mentally rehearsed.

Unfortunately, although it's all-too-normal to listen to an inner critic tell you how undeserving and untalented you are, it may be initially uncomfortable for you to listen to an inner cheerleader and ally advise you about how successful you can be. But stick with it. It just takes faith and practice.

How will you communicate with one another while in your imaginary safe place? Some people talk, mentally, in the same way they might with a friend in reality. Or they share mental thoughts and feelings. Others derive a strong knowledge or a sense about what their Mentors communicate. Another useful approach is too simply allow thoughts to come into your mind as you sit in your supportive Mentor's presence, knowing you can examine the validity of those thoughts later. Experiment a little.

If the communications seem vague at first, don't stress. Open your senses of touch, smell, sound, and sight to this ally. The messages will become more clear with practice—another reason to experience each module several times. Also, as with your Future Self, a clear mental picture isn't necessary. Instead, you can create an underlying perception of your inner Mentor's guidance. This unseen image provides positive feedback and counsel when you relax and listen. Again, practice helps.

As soon as you complete a Module 2 session, make notes of any information and advice you received. Ask yourself three questions before following any advice accepted from your Mentor.

1. *Would following the advice be in my best interest?*
   Let's say you're advised to call your former boss and give him or her a piece of your mind. Consider it carefully. This information sounds as if it may originate from a part of you that is feeling unresolved anger or resentment. Remember that a prospective employer may call your former boss to provide a reference for you. Therefore, following this advice may not be in your best interest.

2. *Is the advice in harmony with my highest goals and principles?*
   Do your highest goals and principles provide for giving people a piece of your mind? If not, the answer is no.

3. *Would it harm anyone?*
   Well, telling off your old boss could harm you, as I said, and possibly your boss as well.

In this scenario, I would send that Mentor away and ask for your wisest Mentor to appear instead. Remember, you are always in control.

The script for Module 2 of the MIT program follows. Remember, execute it three times over at least three days. You may want to return to chapter 3 first and review how to make the best use of the scripts.

Module 2 Script: Relaxation, Mentally Rehearsing a Job Interview, Meeting Your Mentor

Find a comfortable position. . . . Gently close your eyes. . . . Begin by focusing on your breathing—inhaling deeply and exhaling fully. . . . Allow your abdomen to expand and contract as you breathe deep into your diaphragm. . . . And again . . . breathing in relaxation . . . and breathing out any tension in your body. . . . Inhale . . . exhale . . . relaxing more and more . . . becoming more calm with every breath. . . . Imagine any distracting thoughts drifting away. . . . For the moment, your mind is still . . . feeling calm and relaxed now . . . inhaling deeply . . . and exhaling.

Enjoy these few moments in peaceful relaxation. . . . Notice the heaviness as your muscles begin to relax. . . . As I count down from ten to one, allow yourself to become more and more relaxed. . . . Imagine all the anxiety flowing out of you, as you relax deeper and deeper. . . . Ten, nine, eight, going deeper, seven, six, five, four, going even deeper, three, two, one. . . . Very good. . . . Allow these feelings of relaxation to spread through your body. . . . You may notice a warm, heavy feeling coming over you—a sign of deep relaxation.

Now move your attention to your feet. . . . Feel all the muscles in your feet and toes slowly relax and begin to feel very loose and warm. . . . Allow the relaxation to spread into your calves as these muscles begin to feel loose, warm, and heavy. . . . Now release the tension in your knees. . . . Now feel your thigh muscles begin to relax, all the tension releasing down, out of your feet, and into the earth. . . . This relaxing, peaceful feeling is a gift you are giving to yourself.

Now focus on your hips and abdomen. . . . Feel all the muscles loosening and relaxing. . . . Release any tension held there, allowing it to flow down and out of your body. . . . Now your back muscles are loosening, feeling warm. . . . Your neck and shoulders, a favorite place to hold burdens are loosening and releasing any knots blocking you. . . . Continue to relax as you go deeper . . . and deeper.

Move your attention to your arms, your upper and lower arms, and your hands. . . . Let go of any burdens and responsibilities. You can pick them up again later. . . . Sense your

*hands relaxing and warming as the tension flows out through your
fingers. . . . Now focus on your jaw. . . . Sense it becoming loose
and relaxed. . . . Now your face is relaxing, feeling warm and heavy
. . . all the muscles around your eyes, relaxing . . . all around your
head, loosening and relaxing. . . . Feel the muscles releasing their
knots, the anxiety and tension flowing down and out.*

*Now, take a few moments to scan through your body, noting
any remaining tension. . . . Release it now and let it flow down . . .
and out. Allow yourself to enjoy this relaxation and peacefulness.*

*Relax even deeper. . . . Allow your mind to become calm and
peaceful. . . . Remember, you can send thoughts and feelings drifting
away. . . . Focus on your feelings of deep, peaceful relaxation.*

*Now go even deeper. . . . Imagine yourself in your special, safe
place where you are alone and at peace. . . . Look around your safe
place. . . . Sense the shapes and colors coming into focus, becoming
more and more clear. . . . Listen to the sounds of nature around
you—perhaps gentle waves lapping at the shore . . . or birds
chirping. . . . Notice the fragrance in the air, perhaps the smell of
pine trees or colorful wildflowers. . . . Notice the time of
day—perhaps the soft light of morning or the colorful setting
sun. . . . Feel the earth under your feet, or run your fingers through
the water that might be there.*

*Make any changes you like; this is your place. . . . No one can
come here without your invitation. . . . You are in control . . . and
it feels good. . . . Explore a little, reaching out to anything you feel
like touching as you move. . . . Let any distracting thoughts float
away . . . as you go even deeper.*

*Once again, you move toward the large one-way window,
with its view into your life. . . . Settle comfortably in front of it,
perhaps in a large armchair. . . . Notice a remote-control device
within easy reach. . . . In a moment, you will look out the window
and observe yourself in a job interview or other job-search activity
that demands peak performance. . . . You will be able to stop,
revise, and replay anything you see or hear through the window by
using the remote control to freeze the scene and then rewind and
play a revised scene, watching as you continue the interview or
other job-search activity with competence and confidence. . . . You'll
finally play the entire scene through without stopping, seeing and
hearing yourself give a superb performance.*

*Now begin. See yourself during the interview or activity . . .
noting the interview location, the temperature of the room, getting
a sense of the interviewer . . . hearing the questions asked and your
answers . . . using your controls to revise the scene to your*

satisfaction, and playing the new scene with you feeling calm and confident.... Note the interviewer's positive response to you.... You may find yourself being drawn through the window, actually playing the role of yourself in the scene.... Feel free to do that if you like.... Remember though, you can step out of the scene at any time to stop, revise, and replay it.

During the next five minutes, continue the process.... If you become distracted at any time, simply refocus and continue.... You are in control. (Let the tape record five minutes of silence to allow time for the repetition.) ... And now, replay the whole scenario without stopping.... Allow yourself to be drawn through the window into the scene now, as the star performer giving a top performance ... taking as long as you like.... Now, allow the current scene to successfully conclude (let the tape record silence for thirty seconds).

Know that you've done your best, no matter what the result.... Know that you can face and overcome your challenges and that you'll be wiser and stronger for having done so.... You can do what is needed to reach your goal.... Now imagine yourself moving ahead to the time when you have the new position you want.... Sense it in great detail.... How will it feel to have successfully achieved your goal? Feel those feelings now ... the satisfaction and accomplishment.... Take time to enjoy it and let it sink in (let the tape record silence for thirty seconds).

A slight movement out of the corner of your mental eye draws your attention and, as you look around, you notice someone waiting in the shadows at the edge of your safe place.... You nod in invitation, sensing it's your Mentor and, as you approach one another, you become aware of a radiant light emanating from all around this being and wisdom in those eyes that seem to know you well.... Maybe you recognize this person.... Perhaps it's someone who has been a mentor or coach to you in the past—a parent perhaps, or a respected friend, living now or not.... Or perhaps it is someone you don't readily recognize.... Nevertheless, there is something familiar and comforting about those kind eyes and their powerful presence.

Welcome this Mentor into your safe place.... And, as you find a comfortable place to settle for a while, you may sit silently, being warmed in their supportive, loving presence.... Or perhaps you use this time together for counsel and discussion of your current challenges and opportunities.... Perhaps you receive an assessment of the interviews you've mentally practiced.... If advice is offered and it feels right to you, accept it with gratitude.... It's

your choice. . . . Feel your heart open to the love and understanding
being offered. . . . Perhaps your Mentor will communicate with you
through words . . . perhaps thoughts . . . perhaps images or symbols
. . . or some other unique way. . . . Simply allow it to be what it
is, taking as long as you like to drink it in. (let the tape record
silence for a minute or more)

   Sense the beauty of your own life's journey from this new
perspective, the magnificence of your own growth and
development. . . . Perhaps you see a larger plan, new directions, and
new opportunities. . . . Perhaps your destiny is a choice after all. . . .
And now, it's time to say goodbye. . . . As your Mentor departs,
know that you may both return here and meet again anytime you
like.

   In a moment you will come back to full awareness of the
room where your journey began, feeling relaxed and refreshed. . . .
The count of three, two, one will help you return. . . . Three . . .
begin to return, sense the feelings in your body . . . two, sense the
environment around you, and begin to move around . . . and
one. . . . When you are ready, open your eyes and return, feeling
awake and refreshed. Take a few slow, deep breaths. Stretch if you
like, and enjoy the moment.

After Completing Module 2

When you've completed Module 2 three times, once again rate your
MIT experiences with the following scale.

Evaluating the Impact

The statements listed below refer to your program-session experiences. Using the following scale, from 1 to 7, with "I agree not at all" being 1 to "I agree extremely" being 7, place the corresponding number to the left of each of the following statements.

$$1 \quad 2 \quad 3 \quad 4 \quad 5 \quad 6 \quad 7$$

____ Overall, in my session(s), I felt my emotions deeply.

____ Overall, the images in my session(s) were vivid and specific.

____ My focus and involvement in the session(s) were very deep.

____ My experience of relaxation in my session(s) has been deep.

____ My sessions(s) were highly meaningful to me.

____ **Total your score here.**

The total score amount is to be used for comparison only. You want to see an upward trend in subsequent scores over the course of the program. As your scores increase, expect the positive impact of the program experiences to increase as well.

Remember, the total score is to be used for comparison only. Compare your total score and individual ratings on each item with those you noted after completing Module 1. How have your ratings changed? Are you able to focus more easily now? Are your images clearer than when you began the program? Are you relaxing more deeply? If yes, these are some of the indications that your imagery skills have improved.

Next, complete the following Level of Distress Questionnaire and the Level of Confidence Questionnaire one more time, and total your scores on each.

Level of Distress Questionnaire

The statements listed below refer to your inner feelings in regard to your job loss. Using the following scale from 1 to 10, insert the number that most closely reflects your current feelings and state of mind.

1	2	3	4	5	6	7	8	9	10
Never		*Sometimes*			*Frequently*		*Most of the Time*		

_____ I have trouble focusing on what I am doing.

_____ I feel anxious.

_____ I feel frustrated.

_____ I have waves of distressing feelings.

_____ I am reminded of my job loss often.

_____ I try to ignore my feelings about my job loss.

_____ I feel depressed.

_____ I have trouble staying motivated.

_____ I feel angry and/or resentful.

_____ I have trouble sleeping because I keep thinking about my job loss.

_____ I feel fearful.

_____ Any reminder brings back stressful feelings.

_____ I have troubling dreams about my job loss.

For this final statement, use a 1 to 10 scale but, this time, 1 indicates *Strongly Disagree* and 10 means *Strongly Agree*. Insert the number that most closely reflects your current belief, as is relevant to your job loss.

_____ Little can be done to change my job-related problems.

_____ **Total your score here.**

This score represents your current level of distress about your job loss and is for comparison purposes only.

Level of Confidence Questionnaire

Using the following scale from 1 to 10, insert the number that most closely reflects your confidence in your ability to perform that task.

1	2	3	4	5	6	7	8	9	10
Not Confident			*Moderately Confident*					*Highly Confident*	

I can

_____ manage the demands created by my job loss.

_____ use my social network to obtain job leads.

_____ do what it takes to schedule job interviews.

_____ perform successfully in a job interview.

_____ manage my emotions while unemployed.

_____ see my job loss in a more positive light.

_____ learn something from my job-loss experience.

_____ concentrate my thoughts and efforts on my job search.

_____ **Total your score here.**

This score represents your current level of confidence related to your job loss and is for comparison purposes only.

Most people find a substantial decrease in their overall score on the Level of Distress Questionnaire. This is a sign of closure and a return to emotional health.

Note the statement at the bottom of the Level of Distress Questionnaire, "Little can be done to change my job-related problems." The statement reflects your new sense of control, and the score typically decreases several points or more following the program's completion—a good thing.

It's also usual to find a great increase in the overall score on the Level of Confidence Questionnaire. This reflects regained self-assurance about being able to effectively handle the issues and circumstances surrounding job loss and job search. As I explained in the beginning, both questionnaires were included so you could see tangible documentation of your achievements while implementing the Job-Loss Recovery Program.

If you haven't yet improved your levels on the questionnaires to a degree that feels comfortable to you, go back to the program modules and spend more time with them as needed. As a further aid, the next chapter's discussion of beliefs and blockages may be especially helpful.

After you've completed six sessions, you may want to go back to one or more of the scripts to focus on individually. You can spend as much time as you choose with each scenario. For example, if you have interviews scheduled, you may want to practice them with the mental-rehearsal scenario to boost your confidence and maximize your performance on the interviews.

Congratulations! You've completed the Job-Loss Recovery Program. But many more achievements are possible by using your new MIT skills. In chapter 9, I explain how to bust through the limiting beliefs, emotional contracts, and resistances that can block each of us from achieving our greatest dreams and joys.

Breaking Your Barriers

Some people say, "I'll believe it when I see it."
I prefer to say, "I'll see it when I believe it."

—Dr. Robert Schuller

As you implemented and the Job-Loss Recovery Program, the use of desire, expectation, and imagination helped to create unparalleled success. The program works. Many people have proved that over and over.

Yet you may have personal barriers that block your way. Three tactics can aid in breaking those barriers and achieving positive results.

1. Quickly identify and change your limiting beliefs.

2. Break negative emotional contracts with others.

3. Discover and learn from your resistances.

Quickly Identify and Change Limiting Beliefs

First, examine your attitudes and beliefs regarding work and achieving goals; then change any that limit and impede your success. It's easier than it sounds. Our attitudes and beliefs determine what we think and how we feel. And our thoughts and feelings, in turn, determine the decisions and choices we make. So, if your decisions and choices aren't yielding the desired results in your job search, examine the underlying beliefs. Do they empower you or frustrate you?

Remember when I told you about that old belief of mine, that success in life doesn't come without a struggle? My hard-working parents worried and struggled to make a good life for their children and therefore became my role models for struggle. They became successful business-people in their community but not without struggling through difficult times. Nothing came easily. With no conscious awareness, I listened and observed them, coming to believe their reality was the way it was for everyone. As I grew up, my life experiences consistently validated this belief. My achievements were always preceded by struggle and worry.

Thus, the belief I subconsciously developed as a child shaped the way I viewed and experienced the world. This is how many beliefs are formed.

EXPERIENCES ARE FILTERED
THROUGH YOUR BELIEFS.

We experience reality through the filter of our beliefs. In other words, we unconsciously screen out anything that doesn't conform to those beliefs. What each of us actually experiences is the reality that we believe is possible and true. Other potential experiences don't make it through the filter into reality. For instance, I once knew a man who believed most people were rude and inconsiderate; it seemed to him that only rude and inconsiderate people passed through his life. In truth, however, when a considerate person crossed his path (as I observed more than once), he simply didn't notice. Had he done so, the experience would have challenged his belief that all people were rude and inconsiderate. And none of us wants our beliefs questioned. We want to be right—even to our detriment.

Another lesson learned by one of Spencer Johnson's little characters in *Who Moved My Cheese* (1998) is worth noting: "Old beliefs do not lead you to new cheese" (64). He realized that his new beliefs were encouraging new behaviors. When you change what you believe, you change what you do.

At one point in my thirties, a teacher I admired talked about the critical role of beliefs in human experiences. She said life was never meant to be difficult. Her comments prompted me to begin examining my own limiting beliefs relating to areas of my life that weren't working as well as I would have liked, and I discovered techniques to change them. What a difference it made in my life. That's why I'd like to show you exactly how to do it for yourself.

Exercise: Identify Your Limiting Beliefs

Experiencing job loss challenges personal beliefs. Most Americans believe that life is supposed to be fair, and that hard work begets rewards. When the chair is pulled out from under you, these beliefs in fairness, loyalty, and reward are in question.

You may also recognize some of these common limiting beliefs that can block success: "I never get any breaks," "I'm not good enough," "This won't work," and "Change is bad."

In the following MIT exercise, you will be guided back through a timeline of the past year of your life to help you identify undesirable events and reveal any limiting belief that may underlie them.

Have your Journal handy. Select a location where you won't be disturbed for fifteen or twenty minutes.

Find a comfortable position. . . . Gently close your eyes. Begin by focusing on your breathing—inhaling deeply . . . and exhaling. . . . Breathe deep into your diaphragm . . . breathing in relaxation . . . and breathing out any tension in your body. . . . Inhale . . . exhale . . . relaxing more and more. . . . Imagine any distracting thoughts drifting away. . . . For the moment, your mind is still . . . feeling calm and relaxed now . . . inhaling deeply . . . and exhaling. . . . Allow these feelings of relaxation to spread through your body. . . . Notice the heaviness as your muscles begin to relax.

Imagine yourself in your special, safe place where you are alone and at peace. . . . Sense the shapes and colors coming into focus, becoming more and more clear. . . . Listen to the sounds of nature around you. . . . Notice the fragrance in the air, the smell of pine trees or colorful wildflowers. . . . Notice the time of day—perhaps the soft light of morning or the colorful setting sun. . . . Make any changes you like. . . . You are in control. . . . Let any distracting thoughts float away, as you go even deeper.

Find a comfortable place to recline in your safe place, and close your mental eyes. . . . Imagine you're walking back through a timeline of the past year of your life . . . observing events and results of your efforts as they occurred. . . . For the moment, you're interested in only the unwanted happenings that related to your work life or job search. Start with the present and slowly walk through the past year, month by month. As you notice an undesirable incident, walk a little further back, to the decisions and the choices you made leading up to that work-related situation. . . . Simply observe. Don't become emotionally involved. Take a couple of minutes to do that now.

Now, walk a little further back through the timeline to recognize what you were thinking and feeling just before you made those decisions and choices. . . . Look deeply into yourself and be honest. . . . What were your thoughts at the time, and what were you feeling? Simply observe. Take a minute to do that now.

Finally, what was your most prominent attitude at the time? . . . And what is, most likely, the belief supporting that attitude . . . the belief that, directly or indirectly, could be capable of having promoted the unwanted result? . . . You may consider several possible beliefs before one of them feels most accurate. Do that now.

When you've identified a limiting belief, walk even further back through the timeline, perhaps even beyond a year . . . looking for other unwanted events in your life that originated with that very belief . . . looking for a pattern of three or more events. Do that now.

Know that everyone has limiting beliefs, and that you are on the way to recognizing yours . . . and replacing them with positive beliefs that will support and promote your goals and dreams.

When you're ready, come back to full awareness of the room where your journey began, feeling refreshed and alert. Take a few slow, deep breaths, and open your eyes.

Immediately take some time to write about what you've learned. In your Journal

1. Choose the event or result that impacted you most during the exercise. Name it, and describe it briefly.

2. Write the decisions and choices you made leading up to it.

3. Write about the thoughts and feelings that preceded those decisions and choices.

4. Write the underlying belief that feels most accurate. Use as few words as possible. Be succinct.

Let's use the above process with the following example. Assume you had participated in four progressive interviews with a company you liked. After the third interview, you had been informed that only one other candidate vied with you for final consideration. You knew a little about the other candidate, and you thought they had more impressive qualifications for the position than you. You remember feeling disappointed and deciding they would probably get the offer. They did.

On your paper, you would note the following:

1. The event or *result*: interview rejection.

2. The prior *decision* you made internally: "The other candidate will get the job offer."

3. Your *thoughts*: "Their qualifications are more impressive than mine"; and your *feelings*: disappointment and perhaps fear of failure.

4. "I'm not good enough" is a *belief* that could easily have led to these decisions, thoughts, feelings, and results. You need not make an absolute determination, however, based on one result. Look for a pattern of results before concluding that a particular belief is limiting your success.

Repeat the above procedure until you're confident you've identified all the work-related beliefs that hold you back.

If you like, you can use the timeline to go back even further in your life, to the time you first acquired each belief. It's not necessary to do so, however, because you can always change a limiting belief without knowing its origin.

If you're not sure whether a certain belief is healthy or not, ask yourself:

··• Does it empower or frustrate me in reaching my goals and dreams?

··• Does it make me feel good or bad? Understand that a limiting belief can feel comfortable, like an old shoe.

··• Does it protect me in a positive way or not?

If you decide it's no longer in your best interest to hold on to the belief, then it's time to release it and adopt a more constructive one.

> CHANGE YOUR BELIEF TO CHANGE
> YOUR EXPERIENCE.

Exercise: Changing Your Limiting Beliefs

Once you acknowledge a limiting belief that impedes your positive life choices, examine it. How can you change or reverse the negative impact on your career development? Create a new belief to disprove the old—something that will totally contradict that old conviction. That done, mentally express the old belief in one short sentence. Then, in the first person, express the new belief positively, also in a short sentence, using as few words as possible.

For instance, if I rephrased my old belief, "I can't achieve success without struggle," to "Anything I desire comes to me with ease," I could mentally state: "I now release the belief that I can't achieve success without struggle. And I now believe anything I desire comes to me with ease." Repeat it several times for deeper impact.

If you're thinking, "Changing my beliefs can't be this easy," let me point out that you've just expressed a belief you may want to examine.

I learned a second technique many years ago and have used it successfully over and over again. It is implemented in the next exercise script by the use of pictures and metaphors—both of which are easily understood by your new ally, your subconscious. When you have identified a limiting belief, you will go to your safe place and find your way along a path, into a cave. Deep in the cave you'll find a vast, softly lit cavern. In the center will stand a pedestal holding a book titled "My Book of Beliefs." You will open the book to see a limiting belief written on the page and will then be guided through a procedure to replace it with a new belief of your choice. Give it a try.

Find a comfortable position. . . . Gently close your eyes. Begin by focusing on your breathing—inhaling deeply . . . and exhaling fully. . . . Breathe deep into the diaphragm . . . breathing in relaxation . . . and breathing out any tension in your body. . . . Inhale . . . exhale . . . relaxing more and more. . . . Imagine any distracting thoughts drifting away. . . . For the moment, your mind is still . . . feeling calm and relaxed now . . . inhaling deeply . . . and exhaling. . . . Allow these feelings of relaxation to spread through your body. . . . Notice the heaviness as your muscles begin to relax.

Imagine yourself in your special, safe place where you are alone and at peace. . . . Sense the shapes and colors coming into focus, becoming more and more clear. . . . Listen to the sounds of nature around you. . . . Notice the fragrance in the air, the smell of pine trees or colorful wildflowers.... Notice the time of day, perhaps the soft light of morning or the colorful setting sun.... Make any changes you like.... You are in control.... Let any distracting thoughts float away, as you go even deeper.

Begin walking along a winding path that you hadn't seen before.... As you round a bend, come to the mouth of a cave that seems to beckon you inside.... Curious, you walk deep into the cave ... toward a soft glow ahead ... and come to a vast cavern, softly lit by candles all around.... Notice a pedestal standing in the center of the room.... On it sits a large, dusty book.... The cover reads, "My Book of Beliefs."

Walk over to the book and open it to a page on which is written an old belief you intend to release.... Pick up a black marking pen from a small table by the pedestal, and draw a large X on the page over the words.... Put the marker down and tear out the page.... Then rip the page into pieces and burn them in a nearby receptacle.... Feel the freedom and exhilaration of finally releasing the belief.

Look back at the book. Behind the ripped page you tore out is a blank page.... Pick up the marker and sense the satisfaction of writing your new belief on the page.... Mentally read it aloud in the candlelit cavern.... Feel its impact and allow it to sink in.... Now close the book.... Know that you have replaced an old, negative belief with a new, positive one.... Allow it to be done.

When you are ready, come back to awareness of the room where your journey began, feeling refreshed and alert. Take a few slow, deep breaths, and open your eyes.

Can you really let go of an old belief and adopt a new one that easily? You decide. *Conscious beliefs are always a choice.*

Break Negative Emotional Contracts with Others

Another tactic to break your emotional barriers is to examine any undesirable emotional contracts you may have made with others in your younger, more impressionable years.

Throughout childhood and early-adult years, people often unconsciously make agreements with others they depend upon, such as parents and siblings. It's done instinctively and out of self-preservation.

They might be contracts of love, contracts of anxiety and worry, or contracts of hate and hurt. These unwritten contracts often render us unable to use our tools of manifestation—desire, imagination, and expectation—to our fullest potential.

Contracts of love are often motivated out of a desire to hold on to the love of parents. As a way to ensure that we get our parents' love, we fulfill their desires, not ours. I once had a client, Linda, who followed in her father's footsteps by getting into sales. From adolescence on, her father, a successful sales manager, had strongly encouraged her in that direction. Wanting very much to please him, Linda sought and accepted a sales position as soon as she graduated from college. Although unaware of it at the time, she had made an emotional contract with her father that went something like this: "I'll become the person you want me to be and, in return, you'll always love and accept me." She attempted to fulfill her father's desires for her, never asking herself what her own desires might be.

Linda did well enough in sales for a few years, but her heart was not in it. When a layoff followed a company merger, she immediately began seeking another sales position. But she always found something wrong. She didn't like the product, the compensation wasn't good enough, they didn't offer the right territory, or she simply didn't get the offer. I asked Linda how she happened to become interested in sales and she blurted out, "I was never interested in sales." She seemed surprised at her own response, and as we talked further, Linda realized she had never been interested in any other vocation, either. As long as she could remember, she'd accepted that she would have a sales career. She had allowed her father to choose for her. When she related the story to me, she felt anger toward him. Later, she recognized her own willingness to accept the choice and turned her anger inward.

Before she could move on to success in fully gaining freedom of choice, Linda had to first break her emotional contract with her father and resolve the anger and forgive both her father and herself. Once she had done that, she gained the freedom to move in new directions.

Ask yourself whose desires you attempt to fulfill. Yours or someone else's?

Other emotional contracts include a parental promise or a societal obligation. For example you may have internalized a promise you once made to your father: "Out of respect and love for you, I will never become more successful than you." If this feels very familiar, you may have to break a similar agreement to achieve the level of success you want.

To determine what emotional contracts you may harbor, evaluate your happiness and feelings of success prior to losing your job. Did you feel misdirected or unsatisfied? If so, why? Look beyond the obvious. Look for consistent work patterns rather than simply at your last position.

Honestly examine your relationships with parents and siblings. And, if you feel you might have a work-related emotional contract, then you probably do. Keep in mind that I'm talking about limiting and undesirable contracts, not the kind that spur you on to success and fulfillment.

Exercise: Breaking Negative Emotional Contracts

When you discover a contract you want to break, do it with ease and sensibility. Here's how: In the following MIT script, you will imagine severing a visible negative connection that you've emotionally contracted with someone. As always, select a location where you won't be disturbed.

Find a comfortable position. . . . Gently close your eyes. . . . Begin by focusing on your breathing . . . inhaling deeply . . . and exhaling fully. . . . Breathe deep into your diaphragm . . . breathing in relaxation . . . and breathing out any tension in your body. . . . Inhale . . . exhale . . . relaxing more and more. . . . Imagine any distracting thoughts drifting away. . . . For the moment, your mind is still . . . feeling calm and relaxed now . . . inhaling deeply . . . and exhaling. . . . Allow these feelings of relaxation to spread through your body. . . . Notice the heaviness, as your muscles begin to relax.

Imagine yourself in your special, safe place where you are alone and at peace. . . . Sense the shapes and colors coming into focus, becoming more and more clear. . . . Listen to the sounds of nature around you. . . . Notice the fragrance in the air, the smell of pine trees or colorful wildflowers. . . . Notice the time of day, perhaps the soft light of morning or the colorful setting sun. . . .

Make any changes you like. . . . You are in control. . . . Let any distracting thoughts float away as you go even deeper.

Think of the person with whom you want to break the emotional contract . . . and think about the contract itself. . . . Has it helped you in some way? . . . If so, how? . . . Perhaps you did receive more love and now feel grateful, as a result. . . . Or has it impeded your growth and success? . . . If it has, forgive yourself for making the agreement in the first place. . . . You did the best you could at the time. . . . Feel your commitment to break this contract that is no longer in your best interest.

Now invite into your safe place the person with whom you made that agreement so long ago. . . . This person will come, whether currently living or not. . . . Sense them tentatively walking toward you, silently standing a comfortable distance in front of you. . . . Notice a visible connection between you, one you never saw before, emanating from somewhere in your body and stretching across and into the body of the person in front of you. . . . Perhaps it's made of string or cord. . . . It doesn't matter.

If you'd like to say something to this person, do so now. . . . Perhaps you say that although you still feel love, it's time to free yourself from the limiting emotional contract you made so long ago.

Now pick up a pair of scissors that lies nearby, and cut easily through the connecting substance. . . . Watch as the person standing in front of you floats up . . . and fades into the distance. . . . Know now that a limiting emotional contract binding you together no longer exists . . . and you may now freely continue a relationship with that person or not, as you choose.

Think what your life will be like without this blocking emotional contract. . . . What new choices can you make? . . . In what new ways can you apply your skills? . . . Feel the sense of freedom.

When you are ready, come back to awareness of the room where your journey began, feeling refreshed and alert. Take a few slow, deep breaths, and enjoy the moment.

Repeat the exercise with each emotional contract you have. You'll discover that it works well. In fact, you may find that the real person with whom you've broken the contract will actually recognize something is different right away. I know a woman who broke an emotional contract in this manner with her mother—to whom she hadn't spoken in many months. The very next day she received a phone call from her mother, demanding to know what had happened!

Discover and Learn from Your Resistances

The third tactic you can use to create greater success is to recognize and learn about your own resistances to change. You may unconsciously resist the very change you consciously want. In other words, you may say you want change but act as if don't. Why would you do that?

Resistances are psychological defenses or barriers that protect us from thoughts or feelings that may be too difficult to tolerate. Being resistant is not bad or wrong. Unconscious defenses help shut off past, unresolved grief, fear, and other emotions to prevent them from interfering with normal, day-to-day functions. The problem arises when defenses strengthen to the point of barricading a change you really want.

For example, you may subconsciously resist using the techniques offered by this Job-Loss Recovery Program. A part of you may object to the program or to continuing on your current path.

Whatever your underlying resistances, you will want to learn to recognize them in order to determine what to do about them.

Resistances take many forms, but you may be experiencing one if you

- Don't act on one or more of the insights you gain while implementing the Job-Loss Recovery Program

- Feel unusually anxious or uncomfortable while implementing the program

- Do only the relaxation segment of the program

- Skip over the emotional-closure scenario of the program

- Experience extreme difficulty with any of the program's scenarios

- Allow everything else to take priority over your participation in the program

Exercise: Learning from Your Resistance

In the following MIT scenario, you will converse with an image of your resistance and explore why it might be there and how it got there. What could it be protecting you from? What does it need in order to allow the change you want? I adapted the exercise from a script by Dr. Martin Rossman in *Guided Imagery for Self-Healing* (2000).

As always, select a location where you won't be disturbed.

Find a comfortable position.... Gently close your eyes.... Begin by focusing on your breathing ... inhaling deeply ... and exhaling fully.... Breathe deep into your diaphragm ... breathing in relaxation ... and breathing out any tension in your body.... Inhale ... exhale ... relaxing more and more.... Imagine any distracting thoughts drifting away.... For the moment, your mind is still ... feeling calm and relaxed now ... inhaling deeply ... and exhaling. Allow these feelings of relaxation to spread through your body.... Notice the heaviness as your muscles begin to relax.

Imagine yourself in your special, safe place where you are alone and at peace.... Sense the shapes and colors coming into focus, becoming more and more clear.... Listen to the sounds of nature around you.... Notice the fragrance in the air, the smell of pine trees or colorful wildflowers.... Notice the time of day, perhaps the soft light of morning or the colorful setting sun.... Make any changes you like.... You are in control.... Let any distracting thoughts float away as you go even deeper.

Find the spot in your safe place where you feel most calm, most aware, and become comfortable in that spot.... Sense the quiet calm you feel here.

When you're ready, ask yourself if any element of you has an objection to or concern about your continuing on the path of recovery with the Job-Loss Recovery Program or with your current job search.... Simply ask, quietly listen, and wait for an answer.

If there is no response, begin to imagine yourself taking the next step in the Job-Loss Recovery Program or job search.... Invite any element of you that may have an objection to appear in your safe place so you can understand its concerns.

Watch as an image forms to represent this element of you.... It may look like you or not.... Thank the image for revealing itself ... and ask it to share its objections with you, in a way you can understand.... Ask any questions you may have, to clarify its concerns (pause).

Think about what you are learning from this element of yourself.... Does it make sense to you? ... Does the image appear fearful or angry? ... Why? ... Ask it what it needs to drop its opposition to your goals.... Listen to the answer (pause).

Invite your Mentor to join you, and welcome them into your safe place.... Tell your Mentor about the objections of this element of yourself.... Perhaps your Mentor can suggest some ways to meet its needs and free you to move ahead unobstructed.... Listen closely to your Mentor's ideas and guidance.... Ask any questions you may have.... The image wants to have its needs met, and it also wants to be on your team rather than the opposition's.

Share with the image the suggestions that feel reasonable to you.... Can its needs be met in these ways? ... Watch and listen for a response.... If the answer is yes, imagine implementing the suggested actions ... with a successful outcome.

If no ideas are forthcoming or accepted, ask both the element of yourself and your Mentor if they would search the unconscious for creative solutions ... and meet again in a few days to discuss the new ideas.... Arrange a meeting time.

When you're ready, come back to awareness of the room where your journey began, feeling refreshed and alert. Take a few slow, deep breaths, and enjoy the moment.

Immediately take some time to write about what you've learned.

What was the image like? Were you able to recognize your resistive self? If so,

··• Could you relate to its objections?

··• Do you feel you can remedy them well enough, and will you take action to do that?

··• What actions will you take?

··• What did you learn from the experience?

Remain alert for ideas and insights that may come to you over the next few days as you go about your daily activities. Above all, don't judge yourself for having inner objections to your success. It's perfectly normal for a part of you to resist, and becoming aware of the conflicting emotions is, in itself, taking a positive step. But now that you are aware of your objections, you may be able to make some new allies of the different elements of yourself.

In her audiotape program, *How to Live the Life You Love* (1994), Barbara Sher presents an interesting alternative concept designed to deal with resistance. Her idea is to bypass your resistance, no matter what its origin or makeup. Sher suggests breaking up the task or project into small, palatable units, making it a comfortable process and thereby less resistive.

For instance, if you find yourself procrastinating in doing the Job-Loss Recovery Program modules, take the following steps:

1. First, sit or recline comfortably for three or four minutes while slowing your breathing and imagining something relaxing, such as walking on a deserted beach. If you have difficulty maintaining the process for that long, start with one or two minutes and gradually extend the time over a few days.

2. Implement this process on a planned schedule in order to develop the habit of doing a little something from the program every day.

3. After you've worked up to four minutes, move to the program's relaxation script and complete the full-body relaxation, without the safe place portion, once a day for two or three days.

4. Then add the safe place to your routine.

5. You should then be ready to add the program modules as described in this book.

You get the idea. The key is to start small, which encourages participation. It's important to be comfortable with the process and not overwhelmed by it.

To sum up:

••• You've learned to identify and change the limiting beliefs that block your success.

••• You can now recognize and break negative emotional contracts with others.

••• You can work in positive ways with your resistances.

You can now break the barriers that have kept you from the level of success you want and have learned to deal effectively with any new ones that might arise in the future. Congratulations!

CHAPTER 10

Your New Vision: Making a Living with No Emotional Barriers

Go confidently in the direction of your dreams.
Live the life you have imagined.

—Henry David Thoreau

Review Your Accomplishments

Let's take stock of how far you've come since first opening this book. You've learned how to use MIT to

··➡ Relax and manage stressful symptoms

··➡ Reach closure on the loss of your job

··➡ Increase confidence and self-esteem

··➡ Improve job-search performance

··➡ Renew hope and build resilience

··➡ Identify and change beliefs that limit success

··➡ Break unwanted emotional contracts with others

··➡ Discover and work with your resistances

··· Use desire, expectation, and imagination to promote success in all you do.

You're now prepared to land the job of your choice, quickly and easily.

Create a New Vision for Your Life

What if every worker in the world had these new skills? Can you imagine what the world would be like if billions of people could quickly process and resolve all their emotional baggage, if billions could dissolve their inner barriers to success and happiness in addition to the emotional obstructions between themselves and others?

New realities have always started with dreams and visions. What are yours? *Allow yourself to dream.*

Think of every person as a pebble dropped in a lake. No matter where in the lake the pebble is dropped, it creates ripples that span out in all directions and are felt throughout the lake to every shore. In the same way, the actions we take as individuals create impact that is felt, directly or indirectly, by people we don't even know. The dreams you dream, with desire and expectation of success, will attract opportunities to manifest.

> NEW REALITIES BEGIN WITH DREAMS AND VISIONS.

John Lennon must have known about the power of the imagination when he wrote the lyrics: "Imagine all the people living life in peace. You may say I'm a dreamer, but I'm not the only one. I hope someday you'll join us, and the world will be as one."

Exercise: Personal Vision

I have one final exercise for you. I will get you started but, for the most part, you will do this one on your own, without a script. I want you to be as creative as possible, letting your imagination go where it will.

Now, let's get started. Get comfortable, close your eyes, breathe deeply, and relax your body and mind, as you have learned to do. Go to your safe place or not, as you prefer. Imagine yourself engaged in appealing work, and picture the emotionally healthy lives of your business associates (both superiors and colleagues). Have some fun with it. Perhaps everyone has learned about the power of MIT. They have learned how to rid themselves of emotional baggage in other ways, at the very least. What would working relationships be like without the interference of old wounds? Would managers and executives—perhaps you included—want to control and dominate others when their own pain has been healed, and when they have enthusiastic support from coworkers?

How would mergers and downsizing be handled in your personal vision? What's the best way you can come up with to handle layoffs, should they occur? Challenge your creative mind and heart to come up with possibilities and scenarios that could meet the needs of companies and employees alike.

Even if you don't expect a change in corporations' procedures, pretend it will happen. Strong desire, coupled with the use of the imagination to dream, will augment expectation. And when these three power tools are plugged in and working together, you just might get what you asked for, especially when many people are dreaming similar dreams.

In conclusion, I encourage you to continue to use the new skills you've learned. Use them to land the job of your dreams, and continue to use them to create success and happiness in your new life at work. You have the tools you need—now it's up to you to make them work for you.

Mental Image Technology Scripts: Individual Program Scenarios

If you selected the alternate program structure (Choice B), you will use the following five MIT scripts to implement the Job-Loss Recovery Program. Begin each session with the Basic Relaxation Skills script that appears first. Follow that with one of the four succeeding script scenarios in the order given. You may want to review the section in chapter 6 to see exactly how each session is organized. Remember to space your twelve sessions over twelve or more days.

As you read through the scripts, mentally or aloud, read slowly, and pause where you see the dots (. . .) to experience the suggested imagery. Follow a similar procedure, reading aloud, to customize and record the scripts.

Script: Basic Relaxation Skills

Find a comfortable position. . . . Gently close your eyes. Begin by focusing on your breathing—inhaling deeply . . . and exhaling fully. . . . Allow your abdomen to expand and contract as you breathe deep into your diaphragm. . . . And again . . . breathing in relaxation . . . and breathing out any tension in your body. . . . Inhale . . . exhale . . . relaxing more and more . . . becoming more calm with every breath . . . Imagine any distracting thoughts drifting away. . . . For the moment, your mind is still . . . feeling calm and relaxed now . . . inhaling deeply . . . and exhaling.

Enjoy these few moments in peaceful relaxation. . . . Notice the heaviness as your muscles begin to relax. . . . As I count down from ten to one, allow yourself to become more and more relaxed. . . . Imagine all the anxiety flowing out of you as you relax deeper and deeper. . . . Ten, nine, eight, going deeper, seven, six, five, four, going even deeper, three, two, one. . . . Very good. . . . Allow these feelings of relaxation to spread through your body. . . . You may notice a warm, heavy feeling coming over you, a sign of deep relaxation.

Now move your attention to your feet. . . . Feel all the muscles in your feet and toes slowly relax and begin to feel very loose and warm. . . . Allow the relaxation to spread into your calves as these muscles begin to feel loose, warm, and heavy. . . . Now release any tension you feel in your knees. . . . Now feel your thigh muscles begin to relax, all the tension releasing down, out of your feet and into the earth. . . . This relaxing, peaceful feeling is a gift you're giving to yourself.

Now focus on your hips and abdomen. . . . Feel all the muscles loosening and relaxing. . . . Release any tension held there, allowing it to flow down and out of your body. . . . Now your back muscles are loosening, feeling warm. . . . Your neck and shoulders, a favorite place to hold burdens, are loosening and releasing any knots blocking you. . . . Continue to relax as you go deeper and deeper.

Move your attention to your arms, your upper and lower arms, and your hands. . . . Let go of any burdens and responsibilities. You can pick them up again later. . . . Sense your hands relaxing and warming as the tension flows out through your fingers. . . . Now focus on your jaw, sensing it becoming loose and relaxed. . . . Now your face is relaxing, feeling warm and heavy . . . all the muscles around your eyes, relaxing . . . all around your head, loosening and relaxing. . . . Feel the muscles releasing their knots, the anxiety and tension flowing down and out.

Now, take a few moments to scan through your body, noting any remaining tension. . . . Release it now, and let it flow down and out. . . . Allow yourself to enjoy this relaxation and peacefulness.

Relax even deeper. . . . Allow your mind to become calm and peaceful. . . . Remember, you can send thoughts and feelings drifting away. . . . Focus on your feelings of deep, peaceful relaxation.

Now go even deeper. . . . Imagine yourself in a very special and safe place where you can be alone and at peace. . . . You can create your safe place and change it any way you like at any time. . . . Maybe it's a secluded place in nature, such as an ocean beach with gentle waves lapping at the shore, or a forest clearing with the comforting sounds of birds . . . or perhaps a mountain meadow with a gentle breeze whispering through the wildflowers . . . any place where you feel comfortable and safe.

Look around your safe place. . . . Sense the shapes and colors coming into focus, becoming more and more clear. . . . Notice what time of day it is—perhaps the soft light of morning or the colorful setting sun. . . . Listen to the sounds of nature around you. . . . Notice the fragrance in the air. . . . Feel the earth under your feet, or run your fingers through the water that might be there.

Make any changes you like; this is your place. . . . No one can come here without your invitation. . . . You are in control. . . . It feels good. . . . Let any distracting thoughts float away, as you go even deeper.

Script: Emotional Closure

Remember to begin your session with the Basic Relaxation Skills script.

Out of the corner of your mental eye, something captures your attention, and you turn to see a large window somewhere in your safe place. . . . Curious, you move toward it and somehow know this is a one-way window into your world. . . . You can see through it to the other side, but no one can see you. . . . As you look through the window, a scene begins to come into focus. . . . You realize this is you at your former job . . . perhaps when you were told you would be laid off. . . . You choose the scene.

Now feel yourself being gently drawn through the window and sense yourself there. . . . It may seem like a long time ago, or like yesterday. . . . Look around. . . . Listen to the sounds, perhaps of people talking or of computers or other equipment operating. . . . Mentally reach out and touch something in your environment. Perhaps you slide your fingers across a desk. . . . How did you feel at the time? . . . Others, when laid off, have often felt shock at first, then anger or sadness, anxiety, fear, guilt, or even embarrassment. . . . How did you respond? What actions did you take? . . . Or did you do nothing? . . . Are you angry or resentful? . . . If you are, is it toward others? Or perhaps you're mad at yourself for being vulnerable and losing control of your career.

Now invite into your scene, if they're not already there, anyone to whom you want to express your thoughts and feelings without fear of retaliation. . . . Who's there is your choice. . . . Sense them with you, and greet them in your own way. . . . Notice their expressions, their clothing. . . . Remember how you felt. . . . Notice how you feel now. . . . Now set your intention on mentally saying anything you want to say and doing anything you want to do but with no actual intent to harm anyone in reality. . . . As a symbol of your intention to harm no one, sense a protective shield or bubble around you and the other person or persons in your scene.

Mentally say what is on your mind. . . . Don't think about choosing your words carefully. . . . Simply express your feelings. . . . If you feel angry, abandoned, or betrayed, tell them about it as they listen intently to you. . . . If you have mixed feelings, express the ambivalence as well . . . perhaps the sadness of losing contact with friends . . . along with anticipation of new opportunities. . . . You may be surprised at some of the feelings that surface within you. . . . Anything you feel is okay. . . . Simply say and do anything you want. . . . Let it all go. . . . Reach deep within you and release it all. . . . Take as long as you like to do that. It feels good to release what you have been holding onto. . . . You may feel a sense of relief.

Now, how would you prefer to have this person or these people respond to you? . . . Remember, you are writing the script. . . . Listen as they respond in exactly that way. . . . Take as long as you like. . . . How does that feel? . . . Don't label it, simply feel it, allowing the feeling to wash over and through you. . . . Now, if you like, impose upon them whatever retribution you feel is fair and just. . . . It's entirely your choice. . . . Now is your chance. . . . Go for it. You are in control . . . and you're not harming anyone in reality. . . . They do not resist or retaliate in any way. . . . Take the time you need to do that. . . . They may even apologize. . . . If they do, accept the apology or not, as you like . . . perhaps even forgive . . . only when you're ready.

Think of your safe place now, and find yourself there once again . . . perhaps with expanded perspective. . . . Maybe you discovered anger you hadn't realized was there. . . . Perhaps you surprised yourself by forgiving and feel a weight lifting off you. . . . You are learning more about who you are. . . . You know, too, that you are doing your best, and that new opportunities for work and growth are not limited. . . . If one passes, another will reveal itself. . . . You know that challenges are a part of life's journey and that you have the skills to successfully move through and beyond them.

In a moment, you will come back to full awareness of the room where your journey began, feeling relaxed and refreshed. . . . The count of three, two, one will help you return. . . . Three . . . begin to return, sense the feelings in your body . . . two, sense the environment around you and begin to move around . . . and one. . . . When you are ready, open your eyes and return, feeling awake and refreshed. . . . Take a few slow, deep breaths, stretch if you like, and enjoy the moment.

Script: Meeting Your Future Self

Remember to begin your session with the Basic Relaxation Skills script.

Out of the corner of your mental eye, you notice someone standing in shadow at the edge of your safe place.... Curious, you move closer.... This person looks amazingly like you, yet somehow different.... You realize now that this is you at some point in your future, perhaps ten years hence, or maybe even twenty to thirty years from now.... This Future Self represents the epitome of your potential self—the most wise, the most loving, the most happy and successful self you can become in this lifetime.

Invite your Future Self into your safe place ... and as the figure slowly approaches ... coming more into focus ... look for details.... You may or may not see the image clearly—it doesn't matter.... Simply sense the essence and existence of this future you.... Sense the connection between you.... Greet one another in whatever way feels right for you, perhaps a touch or an embrace.

And now look into the eyes of this Future Self, and feel the warmth and loving support coming from one who truly knows you.... See your current life through the perspective of those wise, loving eyes.... Perhaps you're given a sense of what you are truly capable of doing with your abilities in this lifetime.... Take a little time to do that. Allow any feelings and images to wash over you.... You might talk with your Future Self now, and listen intently to the response.... Perhaps you ask for insight into your progress with healing the emotional pain ... or simply experience being in one another's presence.... Take as much time as you need.

Know that you will overcome your current challenges and will be stronger and wiser for it.... Forgive yourself, as well as others, for past failures or disappointments.... Now imagine having received an offer for the position of your choice.... Feel the pleasure of having successfully completed your search ... and imagine yourself celebrating with your loved ones.... Take the time to enjoy that now.

Mentally feel the gentle squeeze of a hand on your arm as your Future Self reaches out to you with a gift.... It may be an object, a symbol, a word, or a thought ... tangible or not.... Allow it be what it is.... If it feels right to do so, simply accept it.... If you don't understand it, that's all right.... For now, it's enough to know that it comes with love.

In a moment, you will come back to full awareness of the room where your journey began, feeling relaxed and refreshed. . . . The count of three, two, one will help you return. . . . Three . . . begin to return, sense the feelings in your body . . . two, sense the environment around you and begin to move around . . . and one. . . . When you are ready, open your eyes and return, feeling awake and refreshed. . . . Take a few slow, deep breaths, stretch if you like, and enjoy the moment.

Script: Mentally Rehearsing a Job Interview

Remember to begin your session with the Basic Relaxation Skills script.

Once again, you move toward the large one-way window, with its view into your life.... Settle comfortably in front of it, perhaps in a large armchair.... Notice a remote-control device within easy reach.... In a moment, you will look out the window and observe yourself in a job interview or other job-search activity that demands peak performance.... You will be able to stop, revise, and replay anything you see or hear through the window by using the remote control to freeze the scene and then rewind and play a revised scene, watching as you continue the interview or other job-search activity with competence and confidence.... You'll finally play the entire scene through without stopping, seeing and hearing yourself give a superb performance.

Now begin. See yourself during the interview or activity ... noting the interview location, the temperature of the room, getting a sense of the interviewer ... hearing the questions asked and your answers ... using your controls to revise the scene to your satisfaction, and playing the new scene with you feeling calm and confident.... Note the interviewer's positive response to you.... You may find yourself being drawn through the window, actually playing the role of yourself in the scene.... Feel free to do that if you like.... Remember though, you can step out of the scene at any time to stop, revise, and replay it.

During the next five minutes, continue the process.... If you become distracted at any time, simply refocus and continue.... You are in control. (Let the tape record five minutes of silence to allow time for repetition.) *... And now, replay the whole scenario without stopping.... Allow yourself to be drawn through the window into the scene now, as the star performer giving a top performance ... taking as long as you like.... Now, allow the current scene to successfully conclude* (let the tape record silence for thirty seconds).

Know that you've done your best, no matter what the result.... Know that you can face and overcome your challenges and that you'll be wiser and stronger for having done so.... You can do what is needed to reach your goal.... Now imagine yourself moving ahead to the time when you have the new position you want.... Sense it in great detail.... How will it feel to have successfully achieved your goal? Feel those feelings now ... the satisfaction and accomplishment.... Take time to enjoy it and let it sink in (let the tape record silence for thirty seconds).

   In a moment, you will come back to full awareness of the room where your journey began, feeling relaxed and refreshed.... The count of three, two, one will help you return.... Three ... begin to return, sense the feelings in your body ... two, sense the environment around you and begin to move about ... and one.... When you are ready, open your eyes and return, feeling awake and refreshed. Take a few slow, deep breaths, stretch if you like, and enjoy the moment.

Script: Meeting Your Mentor

Remember to begin your session with the Basic Relaxation Skills script.

A slight movement out of the corner of your mental eye draws your attention and, as you look around, you notice someone waiting in the shadows at the edge of your safe place.... You nod in invitation, sensing it's your Mentor and, as you approach one another, you become aware of a radiant light emanating from all around this being and wisdom in those eyes that seem to know you well.... Maybe you recognize this person.... Perhaps it's someone who has been a mentor or coach to you in the past—a parent perhaps, or a respected friend, living now or not.... Or perhaps it is someone you don't readily recognize.... Nevertheless, there is something familiar and comforting about those kind eyes and their powerful presence.

Welcome this Mentor into your safe place.... And, as you find a comfortable place to settle for a while, you may sit silently, being warmed in the supportive, loving presence.... Or perhaps you use this time together for counsel and discussion of your current challenges and opportunities.... Perhaps you receive an assessment of the interviews you've mentally practiced.... If advice is offered and it feels right to you, accept it with gratitude.... It's your choice.... Feel your heart open to the love and understanding being offered.... Perhaps your Mentor will communicate with you through words ... perhaps thoughts ... perhaps images or symbols ... or some other unique way.... Simply allow it to be what it is, taking as long as you like to drink it in (let the tape record silence for a minute or more).

Sense the beauty of your own life's journey from this new perspective, the magnificence of your own growth and development.... Perhaps you see a larger plan, new directions, and new opportunities.... Perhaps your destiny is a choice after all.... And now, it's time to say goodbye.... As your Mentor departs, know that you may both return here and meet again anytime you like.

In a moment you will come back to full awareness of the room where your journey began, feeling relaxed and refreshed.... The count of three, two, one will help you return.... Three ... begin to return, sense the feelings in your body ... two, sense the environment around you, and begin to move around ... and one.... When you are ready, open your eyes and return, feeling awake and refreshed. Take a few slow, deep breaths, stretch if you like, and enjoy the moment.

Supplemental Exercises

Exercise 1: Recognizing Your Feelings

This exercise is designed to help identify your specific feelings about your job loss. The script below will guide you through the experience.

Sit comfortably in a quiet location, safe from any disruption. In the exercise, you will set a clear intention to be rid of any distressing feelings. You will send that intention to your subconscious (your ally) by creating an image of surrounding those feelings in a translucent ball, identifying each of the feelings inside it, and tossing the ball away.

As with all the MIT scripts in this book, you may go through the exercise mentally as you read my words, or you may first read the script aloud into a recorder and then actually do the exercise while listening to it play.

Have your Journal nearby to use at the end of the exercise.

Script: Exercise 1

Find a comfortable position. . . . Gently close your eyes. Begin by focusing on your breathing—inhaling deeply . . . and exhaling fully. . . . Breathe deep into your diaphragm . . . breathing in relaxation . . . and breathing out any tension in your body. . . . Inhale . . . exhale . . . relaxing more and more. . . . Imagine any distracting thoughts drifting away. . . . For the moment, your mind is still. . . . Feeling calm and relaxed now . . . inhaling deeply . . . and exhaling. . . . Allow these feelings of relaxation to spread through your body. . . . Notice the heaviness as your muscles begin to relax.

Imagine yourself in a very special and safe place where you can be alone and at peace. . . . You can create your safe place and change it any way you like, at any time. . . . Maybe it's a secluded place in nature, such as an ocean beach with gentle waves lapping at the shore, or a forest clearing with the soft sounds of birds . . . or perhaps a mountain meadow with a gentle breeze whispering through the wildflowers . . . any place where you feel comfortable and safe.

Look around your safe place. . . . Sense the shapes and colors coming into focus, becoming more and more clear. . . . Notice what time of day it is—perhaps the soft light of morning or the colorful setting sun. . . . Listen to the sounds of nature around you. . . . Notice the fragrance in the air. . . . Feel the earth under your feet, or run your fingers through the water that might be there.

Make yourself comfortable somewhere in your safe place. . . . Now let your attention drift to your job loss. . . . Allow your stressful feelings to surface without censoring them . . . all the discomforting feelings. . . . Notice where in your body they are located. . . . But don't dwell on them at this time. . . . Surround those feelings in a translucent ball by simply imagining a ball encircling all uncomfortable feelings.

Sense the ball moving out of your body . . . and see it floating in the air in front of you. . . . Notice the feelings inside the ball and name those you can. . . . Others in your situation have felt fear, anxiety, shame, loneliness, anger, abandonment, and betrayal. . . . You may feel one or more of these emotions or something else entirely . . . and may find it difficult to distinguish between them. That's okay. . . . If you recognize anxiety, look deeper at what lies beneath it . . . perhaps a fear of failure or anger you don't think you should have.

Now take the ball and toss it away, perhaps only a few feet away or maybe high into the atmosphere. . . . Know in your heart and mind that you will soon be rid of these heavy feelings.

Take a couple of deep breaths and focus your attention back to your physical body and your environment. . . . When you're ready, open your eyes.

Now, take your Journal and make a note of the different feelings you could identify within yourself.

Exercise 2: Recognizing Future Possibilities

In this exercise, you'll imagine one of several possible paths for your life. Resist the urge to limit your happiness and accomplishments. Have some fun with the experience, and see what creative ideas begin to surface.

One way to discover your own passion and potential is to look to those you admire. The abilities you envy in others are often the very talents inherent in you, waiting to be developed or discovered. Before you begin reading the exercise script, think of the people in your life and in the world whom you admire. Make a list of them. What is it you admire about each of them? What are the qualities you see that you'd like to have? In what arena are they successful? Is it one you're drawn to?

Next, read the script and follow the narrative instructions, or record it for playback. When you have completed the exercise with one of your imagined future selves, repeat it once or twice with other possible future selves. Imagine what your future might look like if you took a different career direction. For instance, if your first future self was a successful corporate executive, another future self may have become an entrepreneur, having developed an interest or skill into a financially successful business. What would that feel like? Explore your interests.

Script: Exercise 2

Sit comfortably in a quiet location where you won't be disturbed. . . . Imagine being once again in your place of relaxation and safety in nature . . . perhaps a garden with all your favorite flowers and trees . . . or an ocean beach, or a forest clearing. . . . It's a beautiful day, maybe sunrise or sunset . . . with the weather and temperature just as you like it . . . and you can hear the rustle of leaves or waves lapping at the shore. . . . Smell the fragrance in the air. . . . Make yourself comfortable somewhere in this relaxing place.

Now, think ahead to your own happy and success-filled future, maybe ten or even twenty years from now. . . . Get a sense of what you look like, including your health and fitness. . . . What would you like your life to be like? . . . Are you doing work you love? . . . If so, what might it be? . . . Try and get a sense of your colleagues. . . . Or perhaps you are retired and enjoying all the things you never seemed to have time for before . . . family . . . travel . . . maybe even service projects.

Who are the significant people in your life? . . . Sense your family—perhaps grown children—and friends around you. . . . What do you do for enjoyment in this future of yours? . . . Get a sense of the happiness and life satisfaction this future self is feeling. . . . Take as much time as you like.

When you're ready, come back to full awareness of the room where your journey began. . . . Take a few slow, deep breaths, and enjoy the moment.

When you have completed the exercise two or three times, determine which of the futures you feel most drawn to. Then, explore it further and in greater depth, without a script. As you do, notice how deep your desire is for that future, and ask yourself if you actually believe it's possible and if you expect it to happen. Allow yourself to explore dreams and possibilities. (Later you can consider the practical questions about what it would take to prepare for and create that future.)

In your Journal, jot down your feelings and observations after each future-self experience. Which future were you most drawn to, and why? What fears or anxieties came up?

Exercise 3: Refining Your Imagery Skills

If MIT is brand new to you, I'd like to share a few brief exercises designed to sharpen your imagery skills. The Job-Loss Recovery Program will be of greater benefit if you work with these exercises before implementing Module 1.

Intimate involvement in the MIT program scenarios is of paramount importance for optimal success. Remember, even if your predominant sense is not visual, MIT can still have power and depth when you engage all five senses. To demonstrate, try the following quick exercise. In the process, you will be improving your imagery skills. Read through it once to get the idea, and then close your eyes and walk through the scenario.

Script: Exercise 3

First, get comfortable in your chair and take a deep breath. . . .
Imagine yourself in your kitchen, standing over a cutting board,
holding a sharp knife. . . . In your mind's eye, see a juicy lemon
sitting on the cutting board. . . . Notice the yellow color and the
shape. . . . Take the lemon in your mental hand. Feel the
temperature, the weight, and smell the fragrance. . . . Place it back
on the board and pick up the knife. . . . Cut the lemon in half and
notice the sections of lemon and rind. . . . Cut it in half again,
hearing the knife thump the cutting board. . . . Notice the seeds, the
juice, and the scent. . . . Bring a lemon slice to your mouth and
bite down. Suck the sour lemon juice and swallow it.

Salivation is ruled by the autonomic nervous system and is normally out of conscious control. If you salivated when you mentally swallowed the lemon juice, then your own body was tricked, in a sense, into believing you were sucking an actual lemon.

Another exercise to enhance clarity and focus is to simply go to your safe place and practice using all your senses. For instance, you could feel the mist of dawn on your face as you watch the sun come up over the horizon. If there's a lake nearby, you might take a swim or a sail in the breeze. Smell blooming lilacs, pine trees, ocean air, or any of your favorite smells. Listen to melodic birdcalls, whistling wind in the trees, or a foghorn in the distance. Play an instrument you enjoy playing or have always wanted to play. Feel the rough bark of a tree, a velvety flower petal, or gritty sand under your feet. Pick up a little kitten or puppy, and feel the softness and warmth as you pet it. Imagine eating some of your favorite foods.

In *The Mental Edge* (1999), Kenneth Baum recommends the use of six imaginary knobs to enhance visualization. Here's how it works: To begin, think of an exciting and satisfying time you've experienced. For example, you could think back to when you received a job offer you had really wanted, or to a time when you played the best game of your life at your favorite sport. See yourself going through the motions of that event, and allow yourself to feel the exhilaration of the moment.

Now imagine there are six knobs in front of you. One is a zoom lens to make your internal picture larger, one is to enhance the color, and another is to add brightness to your picture. The others control volume, tone, and fine-tuning of the sound. Experiment with them to make your images more clear, detailed, and three-dimensional.

Yet another effective exercise to refine your imaging skills entails sitting comfortably and picking out an object in the room. Look at it and study it intensely—the shape, size, color, and details. Now close your eyes and try to replicate it in your mind's eye. Open your eyes and fill in the details you may have missed. Try it again with another object of a different shape and color. Try this daily or before every MIT session.

Have fun with these exercises. Experiment to see what you find most engaging and what is most challenging. Practice even more to develop and strengthen your less dominant senses.

APPENDIX C

Resources

Imagery and Visualization Books

Achterberg, Jeanne, Barbara Dossy, and Leslie Kolkmeier. 1994. *Rituals of Healing: Using Imagery for Health and Wellness*. New York: Bantam.

Baum, Kenneth, with Richard Turbo. 1999. *The Mental Edge*. Berkeley, CA: Berkley Publishing Group.

Bodian, Stephan. 1999. *Meditation for Dummies*. Foster City, CA: IDG Books Worldwide.

Borysenko, Joan, and Miroslav Borysenko. 1994. *The Power of the Mind to Heal*. Carson, CA: Hay House.

Fanning, Patrick. 1994. *Visualization for Change*. Oakland, CA: New Harbinger Publications.

Fezler, William. 1989. *Creative Imagery: How to Visualize in All Five Senses*. New York: Simon & Schuster.

Moyers, Bill. 1993. *Healing and the Mind*. New York: Doubleday. (Based on Bill Moyers's PBS TV series of the same title.)

Naparstek, Bellaruth. 1994. *Staying Well with Guided Imagery: How to Harness the Power of Your Imagination for Health and Healing*. New York: Warner Books.

Peale, Norman Vincent. 1982. *Positive Imaging: The Powerful Way to Change Your Life*. New York: Fawcett Columbine.

Rossman, Martin. 2000. *Guided Imagery for Self-Healing.* Tiburon, CA: H. J. Kramer.

Ungerleider, Steven. 1996. *Mental Training for Peak Performance: Top Athletes Reveal the Mind Exercises They Use to Excel.* Emmons, PA: Rodale Press.

Career Books

Bolles, Richard N. 2001. *What Color Is Your Parachute? A Practical Manual for Job-Hunters and Career-Changers.* Berkeley, CA: Ten Speed Press.

Kennedy, Joyce Lain. 2000. *Job Interviews for Dummies.* Foster City, CA: IDG Books Worldwide.

Messmer, Max. 1999. *Job Hunting for Dummies.* Foster City, CA: IDG Books Worldwide.

Tieger, Paul D., and Barbara Barron-Tieger. 2001. *Do What You Are: Discover the Perfect Career for You Through the Secrets of Personality Type.* Boston: Little, Brown and Company.

Other Helpful Books

Jeffers, Susan. 1992. *Feel the Fear and Do It Anyway.* New York: Fawcett Books.

Tavris, Carole. 1989. *Anger, the Misunderstood Emotion.* New York: Simon & Schuster.

Witkin, Georgia. 2002. *Stress-Relief for Disasters Great and Small.* New York: Newmarket Press.

References

Achterberg, J., C. Kenner, and G. F. Lawlis. 1988. Severe burn injury: A comparison of relaxation, imagery and biofeedback for pain management. *Journal of Mental Imagery* 12:71-88.

Baum, K., and R. Turbo. 1999. *The Mental Edge*. Berkeley: Berkley, CA Publishing Group.

Birkel, J. D., and S. J. Miller. 1998. *Career Bounce-Back!: The Professionals in Transition Guide to Recovery and Reemployment*. Boston: AMACOM.

Dolbee, S. 2001. Peace proposal: Forgiveness may be the path to healing. *The San Diego Union-Tribune*, April 15.

Fanning, Patrick. 1994. *Visualization for Change*. Oakland, CA: New Harbinger Publications.

Jacobson, E. 1938. *Progressive Relaxation*. Chicago: University of Chicago Press.

Johnson, S. 1998. *Who Moved My Cheese?: An Amazing Way to Deal with Change in Your Work and in Your Life*. New York: G. P. Putnam's Sons.

Joseph, L. M., and M. A. Greenberg. 2001. The effects of a career transition program on reemployment success in laid-off professionals. *Consulting Psychology Journal* 53:169-181.

Kubler-Ross, Elisabeth. 1997. *On Death and Dying*. New York: Simon & Schuster.

Naparstek, B. 1994. *Staying Well with Guided Imagery: How to Harness the Power of Your Imagination for Health and Healing.* New York: Warner Books.

Nicklaus, J., and K. Bowden. 1998. *Golf My Way.* New York: Simon & Schuster.

Noer, D. 1995. *Healing the Wounds: Overcoming the Trauma of Layoffs and Revitalizing Downsized Organizations.* San Francisco: Jossey-Bass.

Orlick, T. 1990. *In Pursuit of Excellence: How to Win in Sport and Life through Mental Training.* Champaign, IL: Human Kinetics.

Overholser, J. C. 1990. Passive relaxation training with guided imagery: A transcript for clinical use. *Phobia Practice and Research Journal* 3:107-122.

Peale, N. V. 1982. *Positive Imaging: The Powerful Way to Change Your Life.* New York: Fawcett Columbine.

———. 1996. *The Power of Positive Thinking.* New York: Ballantine Books.

Pert, C. B. 1997. *Molecules of Emotion: Why You Feel the Way You Feel.* New York: Scribner.

Rossman, M. 2000. *Guided Imagery for Self-Healing.* Tiburon, CA: H. J. Kramer.

Ruvolo, A. P., and H. R. Markus. 1992. Possible selves and performance: The power of self-relevant imagery. *Social Cognition* 10:95-124.

Sher, B. 1994. *How to Live the Life You Love.* Audiocassettes. New York: Bantam Doubleday. Barbara Sher Tapes.

Smith, D. 1990. Imagery in sport: An historical and current overview. In *Mental Imagery,* edited by R. Kunzendorf. New York: Plenum Press.

Spera, S. P., E. D. Buhrfeind, and J. W. Pennebaker. 1994. Expressive writing and coping with job loss. *Academy of Management Journal* 37:722-733.

Tracy, B. 2002. *Create Your Own Future: How to Master the 12 Critical Factors of Unlimited Success.* New York: John Wiley and Sons.

Ungerleider, S. 1996. *Mental Training for Peak Performance: Top Athletes Reveal the Mind Exercises They Use to Excel.* Emmaus, PA: Rodale Press.

Ungerleider, S., and J. M. Golding. 1991. Mental practice among Olympic athletes. *Perceptual and Motor Skills* 72:1007-1017.

Walsch, N. D., and Beliefnet (eds). 2001. *From the Ashes: A Spiritual Response to the Attack on America.* Emmaus, PA: Rodale Press.

Witkin, Georgia. 2002. *Stress-Relief for Disasters Great and Small.* New York: Newmarket Press.

About the Author

 Lynn Joseph, Ph.D., is a recognized author, consultant, and speaker. She worked with Fortune 100 companies for many years in managerial positions in the arenas of sales, training, and human resources. She later partnered with an executive search firm. Dr. Joseph then earned a doctorate in psychology and founded Discovery Dynamics Incorporated, a company dedicated to providing people with the mental tools to create new dreams and achieve goals quickly and easily despite setbacks. *Fortune Magazine* profiled Dr. Joseph in its February 2002 issue.

Dr. Joseph survived several career transitions with the help of mental image technology (MIT). What she later realized was that these powerful tools and techniques were not being used in the practical business world. Introducing them became her mission and led to her developing and scientifically testing a career-transition program based on MIT. The resulting breakthrough study was published in the prestigious *Consulting Psychology Journal*, a peer-reviewed journal of the American Psychological Association, and the successful study protocol is the basis of *The Job-Loss Recovery Guide*, as well as the program recording, *The Job-Loss Recovery Program*. Dr. Joseph presented this study at a 2002 California Psychological Association Annual Conference and at the 1999 American Psychological Association Annual Conference.

Author's Note

Recordings of the MIT program scripts in this book are available on our Job Loss Recovery Web site and by contacting us at the address or phone number below.

Lynn Joseph, Ph.D.
Discovery Dynamics Incorporated
P.O. Box 7905
Riverside, California 92513-7905
www.JobLossRecovery.com
Toll Free Order Line: (888) 557-7776

For more information about our products and services, please contact us via the address or Web site above.

Please write to us, at the above address, about your experiences with the program.

Some Other New Harbinger Titles

Your Depression Map, Item YDM $19.95

Successful Problem Solving, Item SPS $17.95

Working with the Self-Absorbed, Item WSAB $14.95

The Procrastination Workbook, Item PROW $17.95

Coping with Uncertainty, Item COPE $11.95

The BDD Workbook, Item BDDW $18.95

You, Your Relationship, and Your ADD, Item YYY $17.95

The Stop Walking on Eggshells Workbook, Item SWEW $18.95

Conquer Your Critical Inner Voice, Item CYIC $15.95

The PTSD Workbook, Item PWK $17.95

Hypnotize Yourself Out of Pain Now!, Item HYOP $14.95

The Depression Workbook, 2nd edition, Item DWR2 $19.95

Beating the Senior Blues, Item YCBS $17.95

Shared Confinement, Item SDCF $15.95

Handbook of Clinical Psychopharmacology for Therpists, 3rd edition, Item HCP3 $55.95

Getting Your Life Back Together When You Have Schizophrenia Item GYLB $14.95

Do-It-Yourself Eye Movement Technique for Emotional Healing, Item DIYE $13.95

Stop the Anger Now, Item SAGN $17.95

The Self-Esteem Workbook, Item SEWB $18.95

The Habit Change Workbook, Item HBCW $19.95

The Memory Workbook, Item MMWB $18.95

Call **toll free, 1-800-748-6273,** or log on to our online bookstore at **www.newharbinger.com** to order. Have your Visa or Mastercard number ready. Or send a check for the titles you want to New Harbinger Publications, Inc., 5674 Shattuck Ave., Oakland, CA 94609. Include $4.50 for the first book and 75¢ for each additional book, to cover shipping and handling. (California residents please include appropriate sales tax.) Allow two to five weeks for delivery.

Prices subject to change without notice.